SMITH'S
WEALTH OF
NATIONS

A BEGINNER'S GUIDE

MARTIN COHEN

Hodder & Stoughton

A MEMBER OF THE HODDER HEADLINE GROUP

Biography

Martin Cohen is a writer, teacher and researcher in the broad area of philosophy. He is currently a Research Fellow in the Centre for Applied Ethics at Queensland University of Technology, Brisbane. His interests are diverse. Together with Harry Nicholson, he emulated Smith's study of 'rhetoric and belles lettres' with a keynote seminar at Sussex University in the 1980s, at which the conceptually fruitful term 'post rationalism' was first coined. In the 1990s his campaigning on water issues and the environment culminated in a 'Smithian' paper for the European Parliament setting out the economic logic of high environmental standards.

Amongst Martin Cohen's other publications are the iconoclastic *101 Philosophy Problems*, also translated into German, Spanish and Portuguese, *Political Philosophy: From Plato to Chairman Mao* (by way of Adam Smith) and the forthcoming *Ethical Dilemmas*.

Orders: please contact Bookpoint Ltd, 78 Milton Park, Abingdon, Oxon OX14 4TD. Telephone: (44) 01235 400400, Fax: (44) 01235 400500. Lines are open from 9.00–6.00, Monday to Saturday, with a 24-hour message answering service. Email address: orders@bookpoint.co.uk

British Library Cataloguing in Publication Data
A catalogue record for this title is available from The British Library

ISBN 0 340 80405 X

First published 2001
Impression number   10 9 8 7 6 5 4 3 2 1
Year 2007 2006 2005 2004 2003 2002 2001

Cover photo from Corbis Images.
Typeset by Transet Limited, Coventry, England.
Printed in Great Britain for Hodder & Stoughton Educational, a division of Hodder Headline Plc, 338 Euston Road, London NW1 3BH by Cox & Wyman, Reading, Berks.

CONTENTS

FOREWORD

Welcome to …

Hodder & Stoughton's Beginner's Guides to Great Works

… your window into the world of the big ideas!

This series brings home for you the classics of western and world thought. These are the guides to the books everyone wants to have read – the greatest moments in science and philosophy, theology and psychology, politics and history. Even in the age of the Internet, these are the books that keep their lasting appeal. As so much becomes ephemeral – the text message, the e-mail, the season's hit that is forgotten in a few weeks – we have a deeper need of something more lasting. These are the books that connect the ages, shining the light of the past on the changing present, and expanding the horizons of the future.

However, the great works are not always the most immediately accessible. Though they speak to us directly, in flashes, they are also expressions of human experience and perceptions at its most complex. The purpose of these guides is to take you into the world of these books, so that they can speak directly to your experience.

WHAT COUNTS AS A GREAT WORK?

There is no fixed list of great works. Our aim is to offer as comprehensive and varied a selection as possible from among the books which include:

* **The key points of influence** on science, ethics, religious beliefs, political values, psychological understanding.

* The finest achievements of **the greatest authors**.

* The origins and climaxes in **the great movements** of thought and belief.

* The most provocative arguments, which have aroused **the strongest reactions**, including the most notorious as well as the most praised works.

* The high points of **intellectual style**, wit and persuasion.

READING THIS GUIDE

There are many ways to enjoy this book – whether you are thinking of reading the great work, or have tried and want some support, or have enjoyed it and want some help to clarify and express your reactions.

These guides will help you appreciate your chosen book if you are taking a course, or if you are following your own pathway.

What this guide offers

Each guide aims:

* To tell the whole story of the book, from its origins to its influence.

* To follow the book's argument in a careful and lively way.

* To explain the key terms and concepts.

* To bring in accessible examples.

* To provide further reading and wider questions to explore.

How to approach this guide

These guides are designed to be a coherent read, keeping you turning the pages from start to finish – maybe even in a sitting or two!

At the same time, the guide is also a reference work that you can consult repeatedly as you read the great work or after finishing a passage. To make both reading and consulting easy, the guides have:

* Key quotations with page references to different editions.

* Explanations of key quotes.

Our everyday life is buzzing with messages that get shorter and more disposable every month. Through this guide, you can enter a more lasting dialogue of ideas.

George Myerson
Series Editor

SPECIAL FEATURES

This Beginner's Guide aims to bring to life the reading of this great work, and to put that reading in context. For this purpose, a number of special features are included in the text:

* *Key Passage Boxes*: Passages from the original text of key significance for the unfolding argument are highlighted using these boxes. Headings are added to aid definition, with bullet points to pick out the main ideas and terms.

* *Clearly formatted quotes*: A distinctive feature of this reading of Smith's work is that it conveys the flavour of the original so closely. Quotations are woven into the discussion, and many are highlighted for clarity of presentation.

* *Extract Boxes*: A small number of longer extracts from contextual sources are presented in extended boxes.

* *Key Definition Boxes*: One of the most important aspects of Smith's *Wealth of Nations* is his introduction of terms and concepts that have remained central to modern economics. Particularly in the later sections of the present Guide, such concepts are identified and defined concisely for ease of reference.

* End Notes to each Chapter: Each chapter ends with a summary of the sources quoted and referred to. These summaries particularly enable the reader to follow the progress of the reading through the sections of the work.

We hope the result will be a flowing discussion that fills in difficult points for you without too much interruption.

A NOTE ABOUT QUOTATIONS

This beginner's guide is designed to be read in conjunction with any of the many popular editions of the *Wealth of Nations* currently available, or with older editions now out of print. The *Wealth of Nations* itself is extensively indexed and compartmentalized and any particular topic can best be located through the table of contents and indexes of the actual works. However, due to its length, many editors have selected only certain parts of the original for each edition, so the reader may find that several supplementary books will be required. In this book, links are offered to topics as and when they appear in the chapters, using the original *Wealth of Nations* chapter divisions which are the same whatever edition the reader may have to hand, giving guidance to specific discussions typically of a few pages at a time. The full title of Smith's work is *An Inquiry into the Nature and Causes of the Wealth of Nations*, but throughout this guide I shall refer to it as the *Wealth of Nations*.

Some popular editions currently available:

* *An Inquiry into the Nature and Causes of the Wealth of Nations: A Selected Edition* (Oxford World's Classics) by Adam Smith, Kathryn Sutherland. Oxford University Press; (1998), ISBN: 0192835467 (618 pp.). Includes generous selections from all five books of the *Wealth of Nations*. It also provides full notes and a commentary that places Smith's work within a rich interdisciplinary context.

* *The Wealth of Nations: Adam Smith;* Introduction by Robert Reich; edited, with notes, marginal summary, and enlarged index by Edwin Cannan. Modern Library (2000); ISBN: 0679783369 (1216 pp.). This edition both clarifies Smith's analyses and illuminates his overall relevance to the world today.

* *The Wealth of Nations* (Great Minds Series) by Adam Smith. Prometheus Books (1991); ISBN: 0879757051 (590 pp.).

* *The Wealth of Nations/Books I–III,* by Adam Smith, Andrew Skinner (editor). Viking Press (1980); ISBN: 0140432086.

❋ *The Wealth of Nations* (Everyman's Library Series) by Adam Smith, D. D. Raphael. Everymans Library (Reissue edition 1991); ISBN: 06794054X (620 pp.). This edition includes generous selections from all five books of the *Wealth of Nations* and features notes and commentary.

Note: With all the above, other editions include hardcover, audio, cassette, e-book (Microsoft Reader) and audio download. There are also many Internet sources.

The Wealth of Nations is also now kept by Princeton at:
http://www.pei-asia.com/THEORY/SMITH.HTM

IN SUMMARY, A GREAT WORK: ADAM SMITH'S *WEALTH OF NATIONS*

Where others saw human society as determined by human decisions and choices, Smith argues that economic forces have a power all of their own. He shows that our political arrangements, even our values, are only a consequence of these subtle forces. Smith describes the 'hidden hand' of market forces and economics that guides all our actions and decisions. Yet there is also a desire for approval by others – which can lead to conflict.

❋ There is a true or 'natural' price for all goods, reflecting the amount of labour required to produce them.

❋ The hidden hand of the market guides decisions better than any government can.

❋ Taxes, monopolies and regulations generally should be minimized – as they interfere with the workings of the market.

❋ There is a fundamental human desire for approval by others – but this may lead to wasteful display or conflict.

❋ Self-interest governs individuals' actions, but their efforts are ultimately beneficial for all.

INTRODUCTION – READING *WEALTH OF NATIONS* NOW

So, what makes the *Wealth of Nations* 'great'? Being popular? Inventive? Or influential? A truly great work has to be all of these – and more. From Smith, we gain a new perspective on human society. Where others saw human society as determined by human decisions and choices, whether altruistic, as in Plato and Locke, or selfish, as in Machiavelli and Hobbes, Smith writes of an Industrial Revolution and argues that economic forces have a power all of their own. He shows that our political arrangements, even our values, are only a consequence of these subtle forces.

In the intervening centuries between Plato and Aristotle pontificating in the *Gymnasia* of Ancient Greece, and the time of the Scottish Intellectuals declaiming in the smoke-filled rooms of the Poker Club, economics appeared rarely and briefly in philosophical and political debates, and then only as a side issue, for its moral or immediately practical implications. The scholastic philosophers commented on the ethics of charging interest and, in the seventeenth century, there was a vigorous debate about the merits of foreign trade. However, only with Smith is economics carved out as a new and separate discipline with new questions, debates and occasionally solutions.

The harvest from Smith's book has been an intellectually rich one. Smith describes the hidden hand of market forces and economics that guides all our actions and decisions. Yet there is also a desire for approval by others – which can lead to conflict.

Later, Marx and Engels adopted his problematic theory that the value of something depended on the amount of labour put into it – the 'labour theory of value' – and then drew revolutionary conclusions about 'surplus value' and 'exploitation'. Marx also followed Smith in distinguishing 'productive' labour from 'unproductive', before going on to derive a parasitical middle class. Smith, conversely, had a high opinion of the 'superior' classes, as he put it.

The aim of this book, then, is to introduce, in an accessible way one of the few undeniably 'great' works, in the English language, of the last millennium. In line with the series concept, there is a detailed examination of the text, akin to a guided reading, relating the work to its historical and social context, indicating and highlighting key ideas and concepts.

The book will argue that the first person to examine the significance and impersonal power of economic forces was not, as is sometimes said, the iconoclastic revolutionary, Marx, in the nineteenth century, but the highly conventional son of a civil servant lawyer, Adam Smith, a century earlier. It will also answer those more popular questions of the kind that made the original work so widely read, such as: What is a fair wage? What gives money its value? And what disasters happen when patriotism and economics are mixed?

Governments and politicians promoting laissez-faire economics have often called upon the *Wealth of Nations* in their support, but actually the book reveals an Adam Smith who viewed capitalism with deep suspicion and combined the celebration of free, self-regulating markets with darker warnings of the dehumanizing effects of profit-centred society. The *Wealth of Nations* is not merely an economics textbook, but rather a more dramatic story, describing the struggle of both the individual and their society for liberty and prosperity.

Smith's political influence is huge – but it might have been even greater. A major part of the *Theory of Moral Sentiments*, his other major work concerning law-making and government, although laboured over for many years was never completed to the scrupulous Scot's satisfaction. Just before he died, perhaps thinking of his friend David Hume's famous epithet about works of sophistry and illusion, Smith stuffed it into the fireplace and 'consigned it to the flames'. Inevitably a book that is centuries old begins to suffer the same sort of fate, so let this new account provide, in a small way, a re-injection of interest and excitement in Adam Smith's work.

1 Adam Smith

This chapter begins by examining Smith's life and other writings, and the themes of his developing thought, notably the notions of empathy and kindness. Some biographical details and descriptions of his life are included but the emphasis is on understanding Adam Smith as a three-dimensional man, and not just as the desiccated supply-side economist of folklore.

ADAM SMITH: KEY DATES

Milestones in Smith's life	
1723	Born in Kirkcaldy, Scotland.
1737	Attends Glasgow University as pupil of Frances Hutcheson.
1739	His friend, David Hume, publishes his *Treatise of Human Nature*.
1740–46	Studies at Balliol College, Oxford.
1746	Smith returns to a Scotland chastened by the Battle of Culloden and the defeat of the Jacobite Rebellion.
1748–51	Smith proceeds up the academic ladder starting with a series of public lectures sponsored by Henry Home on Rhetoric and Belles Lettres, followed with some on Civil Law for Lord Kames.
1752	Chair of Logic at Glasgow.
1752	Chair of Moral Philosophy at Glasgow, including the area of political economy.
1759	*Theory of Moral Sentiments* published.
1764–6	Tour of Europe in charge of the young Duke of Buccleuch.
1767–73	Returns to Scotland to write 'and think'.

1773	In the colonies, the Boston tea party takes place amid increasing colonial strife.
1776	*Wealth of Nations* published to acclaim.
1778	Smith appointed Commissioner of Customs, H M Government embarks on wars with France and Spain of a largely colonial nature.
1790	Smith dies and is buried in Edinburgh. Sixteen folio volumes of manuscripts are burnt by his executors, barring a few short essays that he allows to be posthumously published on 'philosophical subjects'.

THE *WEALTH OF NATIONS*

The first edition of *An Inquiry into the Nature and Causes of the Wealth of Nations,* cost one pound and sixteen shillings, and sold out within six months. Smith's publisher, William Stahern, had just produced another bestseller: Gibbon's *Decline and Fall of the Roman Empire.* It was thought that *Wealth of Nations* was too technical for the popular readership of *Decline and Fall,* but Gibbon himself realized that there was a great strength to be found in Smith's book. It was there in 'the most profound ideas expressed in the most perspicuous language'.

It was there because the *Wealth of Nations* is, despite the title, not merely concerned with economics. It is a much more comprehensive vision of society, and in its pages economics is merely a by-product, albeit a necessary one, of social life. So Smith is concerned not only with money, but with justice and equity. If his findings are nowadays adopted by those of a different disposition, that is not his fault.

A second edition of the work followed in 1778, a third in 1784, a fourth in 1786 and the fifth and final edition, for Smith at least, appeared in 1789, the year of the French Revolution. It has been translated into Chinese, Czech, Finnish, Russian, Serbo-Croat, Turkish and all the main European languages.

David Hume was first to welcome the work with the words:

Euge! Belle! *Dear Mr Smith: I am much pleased with your performance, and perusal of it has taken me from a state of great anxiety. It was a work of so much expectation, by yourself, by your friends, and by the public, that I trembled for its appearance; but now I am much relieved.*

Another scholarly friend, Hugh Blair, commented:

I confess you have exceeded my expectations. One writer after another on these subjects did nothing but puzzle me. I despaired of arriving at clear ideas. You have given me full and compleat [sic] satisfaction and my faith is fixed. I do think the age is highly indebted to you, and I wish they may be duly sensible of their obligation. You have done great service to the world... your work ought to be, and I am persuaded will in some degree become, the Commercial Code of Nations.

Praise indeed – enough even to satisfy a modern-day publisher in search of material for cover endorsements! As to the book itself, Blair opined:

Your arrangement is excellent. One chapter paves the way for another, and your system gradually erects itself. Nothing was ever better suited than your style is to the subject, clear and distinct to the last degree, full without being too much so, and as tersely as the subject could admit. Dry as some of the subjects are, it carried me along. I read the whole with avidity; and have pleasure in thinking that I shall with some short time give it a second and more deliberate perusal.

The celebrated American revolutionary, Benjamin Franklin, then visiting London, and incidentally dispatching Thomas Paine to the New World to start a revolution, recalled how Smith had read each chapter to him and other friends in London, listening carefully to their thoughts and criticisms, before going away, to rewrite and later bring back a new draft for their final approval. But Hume had struck a sour note too, saying that: 'The reading of it requires so much attention, and the public is disposed to give it so little, that I shall still doubt for some time of its being at first very popular.'

Yet by being comprehensive in scope, by addressing contemporary issues and problems, and locating everything is a complete philosophical vision, Smith managed to appeal to that wide audience that Hume thought might prove evasive. The *Wealth of Nations* is not just an inquiry into wealth, but is rooted in the great issues facing society. It grew, after all, out of a series of lectures on the origins of laws that had started for Smith, like Plato 2000 years earlier, with the question of justice. Smith had started by tackling the question through cataloguing the history of law and had continued with the exploration of the nature of ethics in *The Moral Sentiments*, only arriving later at economics, which he says is the hidden law that governs society. Karl Marx, who is sometimes credited erroneously with this insight, described Smith as the Martin Luther of political economy.

Smith is a philosopher in the style of the Ancient Greeks. He is prepared to deal with all types of question, all types of evidence, untrammelled by notions of sticking to a narrow discipline. He is a philosopher, but also a social scientist, an historian and a natural scientist too. He was an admirer of Newton and his method, which he discerned as being very scientific and objective. Smith is acutely aware that any theory he puts forward – just as with any straightforwardly 'physical' theory, such as Newton's – remains just theory, always capable of refutation. His writing is philosophy as a way of thinking, applied to real issues and questions – not philosophy as an esoteric body of obscure knowledge, as it so often is for lesser academicians. Governor Pownall noticed that the system described by Smith was indeed like Newton's: 'an institute of the *Principia* of those laws of motion by which the operations of the community are directed and regulated, and by which they should be examined'.

His method is painstakingly to examine the research and findings of others and then to make new connections, new discoveries from them, proceeding perhaps slowly, perhaps sometimes ploddingly, but always steadily, working as methodically and impartially as the best scientist (or philosopher) might hope to do, examining the evidence and drawing conclusions only where they could be clearly justified. After all, in the words of the Edinburgh Professor of Mathematics of the time, philosophers and scientists alike should start with phenomena, or effects, identify their particular causes and then, through analysis, go on to find the causes of the causes. In Smith's words, philosophy is the science of 'connecting principles'.

In his earlier work, *On Astronomy*, Smith had demonstrated the approach. He attempted to show why each of the great cosmological systems of history were fated to give way to each other. The system of heavenly spheres imagined by the ancients had started out being very simple, but as more and more subtleties in the movement of the stars and planets emerged, matters became unacceptably complicated. The original three spheres for the sun, moon and stars, increased to 27 spheres by Eudoxus's time, 56 by Aristotle's time, and 72 for Fracastero, before having to be scrapped entirely in favour of what became Ptolemy's system of 'Eccentric Spheres'. This in turn had to be modified by Copernicus, Newton and (we might add) Einstein. The *Wealth of Nations* is similarly an attempt to do away with all the complications of earlier economic analysis and theory and produce in its place a single grand unifying theory.

THE AUTHOR AND THE WORK
So what sort of a man was the author of such a celebrated work? As with so many political activists, Smith's childhood was uneventful enough. His father died before he was born, so he was brought up alone by his mother, Margaret, in Kirkcaldy, on the eastern coast of Scotland. The maternal bond was a strong and lifelong one, and the founder of 'laissez-faire' economics always had a caring side.

Smith proceeded smoothly from Kirkcaldy school to Glasgow and then Oxford universities, via a Snell Exhibition that normally led to ordination in the Church. He had a famously low opinion of the English institution, describing Oxford, disgustedly, as a place where 'the greater part of the public professors have, for these many years, given up altogether even the pretence of teaching'. An accusation that still rings true even today. Smith's years in Glasgow were happier ones, spent in the company of tobacco merchants and bankers at clubs such as the Political Economy Club, who provided him with much of the detailed information but not (at least as far as we know) the theories for his work. He was a member of the Philosophical Society; joined the (nationalist) Poker Club, whose avowed aim was stirring things up, and of which James Boswell observed 'They would abolish all respect due to rank and external circumstances', and the story goes that at the very end of his life, an ailing Smith was able to bid his companions after dinner: 'I love your company gentlemen, but I believe I must leave you – to go to another world.' He even founded a new club – the Select Club – for these idle intellectuals, with his friend David Hume, which became for him both an important influence and the most celebrated.

When Smith later became Professor of Moral Philosophy at Glasgow, he was a most scrupulous lecturer, on a range of topics which included rhetoric, ethics, jurisprudence as well as economics, and was not above putting on extra sessions of related topics that students might find interesting or useful. One contemporary described his teaching as 'plain and unaffected, and as he seemed to be always interested in the subject, he never failed to interest his hearers'. Furthermore, by the 'fullness and variety of his illustrations, the subject gradually swells in his hands, and acquires a dimension which, without a tedious repetition of the same views, was calculated to seize the attention of the audience, and to afford them pleasure as well as instruction...'.

In part, this clarity was because Smith, like many philosophers before and since, believed that grammar was crucial to reasoning and manipulating precisely the 'important abstractions upon which all reasoning depends.' This approach inclined Smith to the merits of the 'plain style' wherein, as he put it, 'Words should be put in such an order that the meaning of the sentence shall be quite plain'. Short sentences were preferable to long ones, and the words in them should conform to the custom of the country as defined by 'men of rank and breeding'. Although figures of speech could appear to give life to writing, Smith believed that the very best writing would not need them.

KEY PASSAGE: COMMUNICATION

When the sentiment of the speaker is expressed in a neat, clear, plain and clever manner, and the passion or affection he is possessed of and intends, by sympathy, to communicate to his hearer, is plainly and cleverly hit off, then and only then the expression has all the force and beauty that language can give it. It matters not the least whether figures of speech are introduced or not.

Smith, *Astronomy II*, 12

Smith's actual lectures were split between the private and the public – the latter were the more important for an academic's reputation. However, the special students committed to his charge (for a good fee) still received a broad education at his hands. For one such, Thomas Fitzmaurice, younger son of Lord Shelburne, he proposed: 'He should learn French and dancing and fencing and that besides he should read with me the best Greek, Latin and French authors on moral philosophy for two or three hours every morning.' The professor of mathematics, Smith promised, would teach him Euclid at that time, as he was too late to learn it in the class. And this was the programme of study for the holidays!

Smith's 'public' lecture was given first thing each weekday, followed by seminar discussions the rest of the morning, with additional lectures in the afternoon, finally finishing off with extra tutorials for selected students (as a perk, not a punishment, of course). Not to mention time for the considerable amounts of extra administrative work that he found for himself.

At this time, the accepted rule was that students paid the bulk of a professor's salary in the form of fees direct to the lecturer. The story goes that when Professor Smith had to leave the university just half way through the session of 1764, students refused to accept reimbursement of their monies, saying that 'the instruction and pleasure received' was already more than they could ever repay. Actually, Professor Smith, ever proper, forced the young students to accept their refunds saying, 'You must not refuse me this satisfaction, nay by heavens you shall not!', and thrust the money back into the pockets of the first young man.

Perhaps if the students had known that Smith merely planned a grand tour of Europe in charge of two young dandies, a privilege offered in return for acting as their chaperone, they might have changed their minds. But in any case, for Smith, the leisured life deprived of this teaching and administrative duties was a punishment and so dull that, early on in the tour, at Toulouse, he wrote home that he had decided to write a book 'to pass away the time.' So it was that the best selling work of its time, and one of the most important economic analyses of all time, *An Inquiry into the Nature and Causes of the Wealth of Nations,* came to be written.

THE INTELLECTUAL CONTEXT
The preceding century had seen two pioneering works of economics already. Mercantilism, the doctrine that governments should seek to control trade through taxes and levies, had been advanced in Thomas Mun's treatises a hundred years earlier, a view repeated in Smith's time by his fellow Scot, Sir James Steuart. In France, however,

the physiocrats had come to the opposite conclusion, preaching as Smith would, the advantages of free trade. François Quesnay's *Tableau Economique* (1758) also paved the way for Smith's system by describing the annual flow of payments in the economy from one group to another, with Quesnay distinguishing like Smith four fundamental types of money: rent, prices, wages and profits.

The 'French School' of economists was hailed by Smith as the 'most distinct and best connected account of the doctrine', and the man himself, Quesnay, doctor to the King , as 'one of the worthiest men in France' (not to mention, a 'friend and confidant of Madame Pompadour a woman who was no contemptible judge of merit', as Smith put it in a letter to Lady Scott).

The French held that agriculture and mining were fundamentally the source of national wealth because they alone permitted a genuine conversion of labour into production: other processes, such as manufacturing merely turned one sort of product into another. Quesnay believed that agriculture was the true source of all wealth, as it alone created more than was put in, a genuine surplus, owing to the role of God and nature. Other forms of human activity, merely changed goods from one form to another, consuming resources in order to do so. Smith was highly impressed by this, describing it in the *Wealth of Nations* as 'perhaps the nearest approximation to the truth that has yet been discovered on the subject of political economy'.

Returning to his native Scotland and Kirkcaldy in 1767 Smith wrote to his lifelong friend, David Hume (and indeed literary editor, although neither of these facts mitigated in Smith's mind against recommending against Hume's appointment to a chair of philosophy at one time:):

My business here is study in which I have been very deeply engaged for about a month past. My amusements are long, solitary walks by the seaside. You may judge how I spend my time. I feel myself, however, extremely happy, comfortable and contented. I never was, perhaps, more so in all my life.

Smith's plan was that *Wealth of Nations* should be a companion volume to his other major work, completed some years earlier, *The Moral Sentiments*. This describes 'sympathy' (a better word today might be 'empathy') as the cement that holds society together and uses the idea of 'the independent spectator', who judges our actions. This book had already been something of a triumph. Only a few weeks after its publication, Hume had written to Smith to describe the 'melancholy news' that the: 'Bishop of Peterborough said he had passed an evening in company where he had heard it extolled above all books in the world.' He continued in the atheistic fashion that caused Smith so much embarrassment, 'You may conclude what opinion true philosophers will have of it, when these retainers to superstition praise it so highly...' And another admirer of the book was Charles Townshend. He would prove to be an important influence as it was he who decided that Smith was the professor to take charge of his stepson, the younger Duke of Buccleuch.

A great assistance to Smith in the project was a book by Sir James Steuart called (like John Stuart Mill's more famous work) *Principles of Political Economy* (1767). Further material for the work was found in Lord Hailes's extensive archive of prices (in Scotland, from 1243 to 1561) which, throughout the last year of the 1760s, Smith was struggling, as he put it, 'to give them the last Arrangement.' And, in putting together his economic theory, Smith drew in part, as already mentioned, upon his lectures on 'Jurisprudence', but even in the most rudimentary notes, it is clear that Smith had, in keeping with his method, already identified the fundamentals. Notably, the role of the division of labour in the economy, a theory of price mechanisms, and a doctrine of natural liberty. All that remained for later was to integrate the fine distinctions between the various kinds of economic production (those based on, respectively, land and raw materials, those on human labour and work, and those based on monetary or 'manufactured' capital itself). Similarly, he needed to finalize the details of monetary 'return', in its various forms: rent, wages and profit.

Unfortunately for Smith, try as he might, and clear as the fundamentals appeared to be, the prices did not seem to fit with his tidy and logical system. Rather, 'all the estimated prices of grain among our ancestors seem to have been extremely loose and inaccurate' (letter to Lord Hailes, of Campbell and Skinner, 1982). The struggle continued for not just months, but years. In 1772, as the story goes, an over-stressed and overworked Smith sleep-walked in his dressing gown from Kirkcaldy to Dunfermline, a distance of 15 miles, awakened only by the tolling of church bells in the early morning! At the same time as Smith wrestled with prices, many banks – the Newcastle, Norwich, Bristol and even closer to home, the Ayr – collapsed into bankruptcy. Even the Bank of England was said to be shaking. The collapse in confidence and associated loss of jobs made Smith's labour seem even more important, along with his ambitious attempts to get the prescription for the economic ills of the time right.

One such case of monopolistic restrictions which embroiled Smith was that of the rights of universities to set standards for the issuing of medical degrees – or so they would put it. Smith saw it rather differently. 'There never was, and I will venture to say there never will be, a university from which a degree could give any tolerable security that the person upon whom it had been conferred, was fit to practise...'. Their real motive, in setting minimum requirements, Smith wrote, was simply to 'make more profit'.

A degree can pretend to be security for nothing but the science of the graduate; and even for that it can give but a very slender security. For his good sense and discretion, qualities not discoverable by an academical examination,

it can give no security at all. But without these, the
presumption which commonly attends science must render
it, in the practice of physic, ten times more dangerous than
the grossest ignorance...

Smith adds: 'A degree always has been, and in spite of all the regulations which can be made, always must be, a mere price of quackery, it is certainly for the advantage of the public that it should be understood to be so.' But this was but a side show. Although the *Wealth of Nations* puts education high on the (very short) list of government priorities, the issue that overshadows the final years of work was not of bank insolvency, far less university monopolies. It was the issue of British colonial policy and the rumblings from North America.

After all, as Smith puts it: 'The discovery of America, and that of a passage to the East Indies by the Cape of Good Hope, as the two greatest and most important events recorded it the history of mankind'. Not that he sees the discovery entirely through rose-tinted glasses, writing with unusual passion:

KEY PASSAGE: INTELLECTUAL PASSION

Folly and injustice seem to have been the principles which presided over and directed the first project of establishing those colonies; the folly of hunting after gold and sliver mines, and the injustice of coveting the possessions of a country whose harmless natives, far from having ever injured the people of Europe, had received the first adventurers with every mark of kindness and hospitality.

Undeniably, the availability of land and other natural resources to the colonists, and the political regulations limiting trade to Britain and her colonies, Smith found ideally suited for the rapid development of the New World. This was true even of limitations such as those obliging the colonies to produce raw materials and forestall attempts to manufacture.

> *Unjust, however, as such prohibitions may be, they have not hitherto been very hurtful to the colonies. Land is still so cheap, and consequently, labour so dear among them, that they can import from the mother country, almost all the more refined or more advanced manufactures cheaper than they could make for themselves.*

By contrast, Britain, through the Navigation Acts (which protected trade with the colonies) had skewed her industries and markets counterproductively.

> *Instead of being suited, as before the act of navigation, to the neighbouring market of Europe, or the more distant one of the countries which lie round the Mediterranean sea… the greater part of them have been accommodated to the still more distant one of the colonies.*

Better to follow the clarion call of Free Trade, a call made repeatedly and loudly throughout the work, on the principle that whilst nationalism may dictate self-reliance and allow importation, economics preaches the advantages of specialization and openness. Smith was concerned that his advocacy of free trade and the dismantling of monopolies might cause him to become unfashionably if not unhealthily controversial, but in the event his views on economics proved far less inflammatory than some modest good wishes he expressed by way of an obituary for his old friend Hume, who died shortly after the publication of the book. In particular, the opprobrium was occasioned by his epitaph for Hume that he approached in his opinion 'as nearly the idea of a perfectly wise and virtuous man as perhaps the nature of human frailty will permit'. These wishes brought upon him 'ten times more abuse than the very violent attack I had made upon the whole commercial system of Great Britain,' he wrote bemusedly later.

Indeed, the Government remained so unshaken by the very violent attack, that a year later it even allowed Smith to become, of all things, Commissioner for Customs in Edinburgh, overseeing the charges he had condemned so roundly. Even as Commissioner for Customs advising the British Government on trade policy, Smith stuck to his free market views, self-negating though they then became. Smith even expressed them in a letter to William Eden, the Prime Minister, saying that, 'Prohibitions do not prevent the importation of prohibited goods. They are bought everywhere, in the fair way of trade, by people who are not in the least aware that they are buying them.' He continues in the *Wealth of Nations*:

KEY PASSAGE: INTELLECTUAL PASSION

Her commerce, instead of running in a great number of small channels, has been taught to run principally in one great channel. But the whole system of her industry and commerce has thereby been rendered less secure; the whole state of her body politick less healthful, than it otherwise would have been. In her present condition, Great Britain resembles one of the those unwholesome bodies in which some of the vital parts are overgrown, and which, upon that account, are liable to many dangerous disorders scarce incident to those in which all the parts pare more properly proportioned.

Symptomatic of this disease was the National Debt, which Smith noted was growing at an astronomical rate reaching the shocking level of £130 million in 1775. Most of this was the cost of colonizing the rest of the world, which despite the common-sense view of such expeditions (as profitable plunder), was in fact a ruinously expensive imperial venture.

The only thing to do (and what of course was done to such disastrous effect from the British Government's point of view anyway) was tax the colonies. Smith himself saw this not as an imposition but as part of normal democratic procedures. The taxes should correspond to the services provided by the British, notably defence (the 'liberty, security and property' that the colonialists enjoyed – or rather didn't), and those taxed would then have, as of right, representation in the parliament. (A similar sort of 'union' was offered by Smith to the Irish.) Indeed, Smith foresaw a time when the might of America would increase to the extent that its economy would dwarf the mother country, and the parliament itself would naturally relocate across the Atlantic to be at its heart. 'The seat of empire would then naturally remove itself to that part of the empire which contributed most.'

At the time of the publication of *Wealth of Nations*, this opportunity had become evidently lost. Even for two countries to part, as Smith puts it in Book IV, as 'good friends' leaving warmth and a special relationship was looking unlikely. However, Smith was prescient in his prediction that ultimately, the shared language and origins would bring the two together again.

Smith did have some influence in government circles. He saw Pitt the Younger regularly, and found him an eager audience for his economic theorizing. His ideas immediately found their way into government policy, with new forms of taxation introduced in the budget of 1777 and 1778 and discussion of the advantages of 'free trade' both with America and Ireland. But in general, Smith himself, like other Scottish intellectuals of the time, adopted rather a lofty attitude towards practical matters. Although the Act of Union of 1707 between Scotland and England was still rather controversial, some like Smith thought the advantages of commerce certainly outweighed the political costs in terms of sovereignty. Certainly, it had had the effect of triggering a great revival of intellectual activity in Scotland, and as the Scots were freed from the trivia of government they pursued instead philosophy, economics and creative invention. It was, after all, in the salons of Paris, not in the universities, that Smith had mixed with the 'physiocrats', such as Quesnay.

Moreover, it left Smith free to become a leading light, or at least a regular feature, munching sugar lumps, in many of the clubs of the day. At the dinner parties in London, it is said, the sugar bowl had to be placed out of Smith's reach. A counter-example, of course, to 'laissez-faire'.

Notes to Chapter 1

Smith's life is explored in detail in *Adam Smith*, by R. H. Campbell and A. S. Skinner, Croom Helm (1982).

The role of clarity in writing was described in a letter to George Baird (1763) and the suggested curriculum for the special students is set out in a letter to Lord Shelburne (1757). The letter to David Hume announcing his intention to devote himself to study is dated 7 June 1767.

See Book IV, Chapter vii for Smith's view of the North American colonies and the correct way to run trade to ensure a healthy economy.

2 Human Nature and the Origins of Society

We begin the guided reading proper with a look at:

* Smith's assumptions about the origins of society.

* Smith's theory of human nature.

THE FOUR STAGES IN SOCIETY

In the *Wealth of Nations* (1776) Adam Smith invariably, even monotonously, writes of four stages in society:

* an age of hunters;

* an age of shepherds;

* an agrarian age; and

* an age of commerce.

Smith refers to 'first man' but avoids the 'state of nature', thinking perhaps of his friend David Hume's, attack on the concept. In fact, Smith's perspective on 'savage man' is more like a plea for the welfare state.

Among the savage nations of hunters and fishers, every individual who is able to work, is more or less employed in useful labour, and endeavours to provide, as well as he can, the necessaries and conveniences of life, for himself, or much of his family or tribe as are either too old, or too young, or too infirm to go a hunting and fishing. Such nations are, however, so miserably poor that, from mere want, they are frequently reduced, or at least, think themselves reduced, to the necessity sometimes of directly destroying, and sometimes of abandoning their infants, their old people, and those afflicted with lingering diseases to perish with hunger, or to be devoured by wild beasts.

Society, he says, only begins to need laws and government in the second stage. The 'age of shepherds' is where government commences. 'Property makes it absolutely necessary... Til there be no property, there can be no government the very end of which is to secure wealth, and defend the rich from the poor', as he put it earlier, in one of his 'Lectures on Jurisprudence':

The wood of the forest, the grass of the field, and all the natural fruits of the earth, which, when land was in common, cost the labourer only the trouble of gathering them, come... to have an additional price fixed upon them.

In the *Wealth of Nations*, Smith writes that without property, civil society does not come into existence.

The establishment of valuable and extensive property... necessarily requires the establishment of civil government. Where there is no property, or at least none that exceeds the value of two or three days labour, civil government is not so necessary.

In an aside, by way of a comparison, Smith notes with, for his time, some originality, that the North American Indians, despite having no sense of property, still had a system of collective farming, of agriculture.

However, in the more archetypal 'second stage' of society, animals begin to belong to people, and shepherds, unlike the hunters, begin to be concerned with future planning as well as the present. In seeing the need to protect property as the origin of government, and hence society, Smith is following the earlier English philosopher, John Locke. However, unlike Locke and in a moment of radical insight he sees the process as bearing rather unequally on the citizens:

Civil government, so far as it is instituted for the security of property, is in reality instituted for the defence of the rich against the poor, or of those who have some property against those who have none at all.

Smith has in mind here, too, Rousseau's *Discourse on Inequality* wherein it is claimed that the institution of property is responsible for much misery and injustice, and nothing good comes of it – even for the rich.

Smith shares a great deal of Rousseau's scepticism about the effects of 'progress' on people, but as far as material impoverishment goes, Smith sees salvation in the laws of economics: the market will come to our rescue, we need not rely simply on human fellow feeling. In particular, 'a certain propensity in human nature to truck, barter, and exchange one thing for another'. This trait is 'common to all men', but not to be found in any other race of animals. After all, as he puts it: 'Nobody ever saw a dog make as fair and deliberate exchange of one bone for another with another dog.'

JEAN JACQUES ROUSSEAU (1712–78)

Question proposed by the Academy of Dijon:

What is the origin of the inequality among Mankind; and whether such inequality is authorized by the Law of Nature?

Men soon ceasing to fall asleep under the first tree, or take shelter in the first cavern, lit upon some hard and sharp kinds of stone resembling spades or hatchets, and employed them to dig the ground, cut down trees, and with the branches build huts, which they afterwards bethought themselves of plastering over with clay or dirt. This was the epoch of a first revolution, which produced the establishment and distinction of families, and which introduced a species of property, and along with it perhaps a thousand quarrels and battles. As the strongest however were probably the first to make themselves cabins, which they knew they were able to defend, we may conclude that the weak found it much shorter and safer to imitate than to attempt to dislodge them: and as to those, who were already provided with cabins, no one could have any great temptation to seize upon that of his neighbour, not so much because it did not belong to him, as because it could be of no service to him; and as besides to make himself master of it, he must expose himself to a very sharp conflict with the present occupiers.

But we must take notice, that the society now formed and the relations now established among men required in them qualities different from those, which they derived from their primitive constitution; that as a sense of morality began to insinuate itself into human actions, and every man, before the enacting of laws, was the only judge and avenger of the injuries he had received, that goodness of heart suitable to the pure state of nature by no means suited infant society; that it was necessary punishments should become severer in the same proportion that the opportunities of offending became more frequent, and the dread of vengeance add strength to the too weak curb of the law. Thus, though men were becoming less patient, and natural compassion had already suffered some alteration, this period of the development of the human faculties, holding a just mean between the indolence of the primitive state, and the petulant activity of self-love, must have been the happiest and most durable epoch.

The more we reflect on this state, the more convinced we shall be, that it was the least subject of any to revolutions, the best for man, and that nothing could have drawn him out of it but some fatal accident, which, for the public good, should never have happened. The example of the savages, most of whom have been found in this condition, seems to confirm that mankind was formed ever to remain in it, that this condition is the real youth of the world, and that all ulterior improvements have been so many steps, in appearance towards the perfection of individuals, but in fact towards the decrepitness of the species.

As long as men remained satisfied with their rustic cabins; as long as they confined themselves to the use of clothes made of the skins of other animals, and the use of thorns and fish-bones, in putting these skins together; as long as they continued to consider feathers and shells as sufficient ornaments, and to paint their bodies of different colours, to improve or ornament their bows and arrows, to form and scoop out with sharp-edged stones some little fishing boats, or clumsy instruments of music; in a word, as long as they undertook such works only as a single person could finish, and stuck to such arts as did not require the joint endeavours of several hands, they lived free, healthy, honest and happy, as much as their nature would admit, and continued to enjoy with each other all the pleasures of an independent intercourse; but from the moment one man began to stand in need of another's assistance; from the moment it appeared an advantage for one man to possess the quantity of provisions requisite for two, all equality vanished; property started up; labour became necessary; and boundless forests became smiling fields, which it was found necessary to water with human sweat, and in which slavery and misery were soon seen to sprout out and grow with the fruits of the earth.

[extracted from *A Discourse Upon The Origin and The Foundation of The Inequality among Mankind*]

This 'propensity' is actually the origin of social co-operation. No other species has it. Even if: 'Two greyhounds, in running down the same hare, have sometimes the appearance of acting in some sort of concert, each turns her towards his companion, or endeavours to intercept her when his companion turns her towards himself', the appearance of co-operation is here only an illusion.

The nearest animals, such as dogs, come to bartering is their 'fawning and servile attentions' aimed at obtaining favours or consideration. Fortunately, Smith observes, animals once grown are 'almost entirely independent'. Not so the human animal. 'In civilised society he stands at all times in need of the co-operation and assistance of great multitudes, while his whole life is scarce sufficient to gain the friendship of a few persons.' The plain fact is: 'Man has almost constant occasion for the help of his brethren, and it is in vain for him to expect it from their benevolence only.' He will do better 'if he can interest their self-love in his favour' instead. So, in the words of the most celebrated passage of the book:

KEY PASSAGE: THE VIRTUES OF SELFISHNESS

It is not from the benevolence of the butcher, the brewer, or the baker, that we expect our dinner, but from their regard to their own self-interest. We address ourselves not to their humanity but to their self love, and never talk to them of our own necessities but of their advantage. Nobody but a beggar chooses to depend chiefly upon the benevolence of his fellow citizens. Even a beggar does not depend upon it entirely... The greater part of his occasional wants are supported in the same manner as those of other people, by treaty, by barter and by purchase, with the money which one man gives him he purchases food, the old cloaths which another bestows upon him he exchanges for other old cloaths which suit him better, or for lodging, or for food, or for money...

---

o '*Self-interest*': This remains one of the central terms in modern political debate. For Smith, 'self-interest' is, we note, reciprocal rather than mutually exclusive, as in many later arguments.

He goes on:

> ## KEY PASSAGE: THE REWARDS
>
> *If we examine, I say, all these things, and consider what a variety of labour is employed about each of them, we shall be sensible that without the assistance and co-operation of many thousands, the very meanest person in a civilised country could not be provided, even according to, what we very falsely imagine, the easy and simple manner in which he is commonly accommodated. Compared, indeed, with the more extravagant luxury of the great, his accommodation must no doubt appear extremely simple and easy, and yet it may be true, perhaps , that the accommodation of an European prince does not always so much exceed that of an industrious and frugal peasant, as the accommodation of the latter exceeds that of many an African King, the absolute master of the lives and liberties of ten thousand naked savages.*

o The modern worker has no power directly over anyone. Yet, indirectly, they call upon the services of far more than the ancient rulers could.

In the *Wealth of Nations,* Smith then follows up his earlier theory, set out in the *Moral Sentiments,* that the central motivation of mankind is a desire for approval by others. 'Sympathy', or 'awareness of other's feelings', (we might say 'empathy') explains morality; the division of labour explains economics. 'Sympathy' also creates a social bond. Human beings, Smith explains, have a spontaneous tendency to observe others. From this, we turn to judging ourselves. The moral identity of the individual develops, in this way, from social interaction. A human being growing up in isolation, will have no sense of right and wrong – or any need for the concept.

In the earlier books, he writes:

Were it possible that a human creature could grow up to manhood in a solitary place, without any communication with his own species, he could no more think of his own character, or the propriety or demerit of his own sentiments and conduct, of the beauty or deformity of his own mind, than the beauty or deformity of his own face... Bring him into society and he is immediately provided with the mirror... (TMS, I, iii)

So, *it is self-interest that underpins the economic system.* That 'great Leviathan', as posited by Thomas Hobbes a century earlier, the collective Man, society itself, is otherwise a dumb brute. People contribute to social outcomes of which they had no conscious intention of doing.

THEORY OF MORAL SENTIMENTS

The wheels of the watch are all admirably adjusted to the end for which it was made, the pointing of the hour. All their various motions conspire in the nicest manner to produce this effect. If they were endowed with a desire and intention to produce it, they could not do it better. yet we never ascribe any such intention or desire to them, but to the watchmaker, and we know that they are put into motion by a spring, which intends the effect it produces as little as they do.

(*Theory of Moral Sentiments* (1759), VII, ii)

If the motive is self-interest, this is not in itself to be scorned for:

How destructive so ever this system may appear, it could never have imposed upon so great a number of persons, nor have occasioned so general an alarm among those who

*are the friends of better principles had it not in some
respects bordered up on the truth.*

(TMS, II, iv)

There are four factors determining people's respect for others:
personal qualities, age, fortune and birth. The first is open to
debate, so age is a better yardstick. Fortune, or wealth, is, Smith
notes, a surprising source of respect. Rich people are admired and
benefit in terms of social esteem just by their wealth. Poor people
lose two ways.

*[The] conditions of human nature were peculiarly hard,
if those affections, which by the very nature of our being,
ought frequently to include our conduct, could upon no
occasion appear virtuous, or deserve esteem and
commendation from any body.*

(TMS, VII, ii)

Smith is aware of the possibility of self-deception and curses it as
the source of 'half of the disorders of human life'. If only, he wrote
in the *Moral Sentiments*, we could see ourselves as others see us, 'a
reformation would be unavoidable. We could not otherwise
endure the sight.'

*To judge your own behaviour requires you to, at least for
a moment, divide into two people, and one be the
spectator of the actions of the other. Nature has endowed
each of us with a desire not only to be approved of, 'but
with a desire of being what ought to be approved of'
(which is rather harder).*

(TMS III, ii)

Like Freud, Smith sees moral behaviour as built up in the mind
from the influence of parents, teachers, school fellows (peer

group) and society in general. The conscience acts as a kind of 'impartial spectator', watching and judging us.

Where Freud would allow the unconscious to still lead us astray, Smith makes his impartial spectator similar in role to that of the Freudian super ego, and quite capable of leading us towards the light.

> ... *it is chiefly from this regard to the sentiments of mankind that we pursue riches and avoid poverty. For to what purpose is all the toil and bustle of the world? What is the end of avarice and ambition, of the pursuit of wealth, of power, or pre-eminence?... To be observed, to be attended to, to be taken notice of with sympathy, complacency, and approbation, are all the advantages which we can propose to derive from it. It is the vanity, not the ease or the pleasure, which interests us.* (TMS, I, iii)

THE HIDDEN HAND

The law of unintended social outcomes becomes through Smith's phrase 'the invisible hand'.

KEY PASSAGE: THE INVISIBLE HAND

... every individual necessarily labours to render the annual revenue of the society as great as he can. He generally, indeed, neither intends to promote the publick intent, nor knows how much he is promoting it... he intends only his own gain, and he is in this, as in many other cases, led by an invisible hand to promote an end which was no part of his intention.

---

o The key is in the division of labour.

Smith illustrates the advantages of the division of labour by considering the increase in productivity possible by changing the process of manufacture of a pin in a pin factory. Acting alone, he says, one man could 'scarce, with his utmost industry, make one pin a day', and certainly could not make twenty. But if the work can be divided up:

> *...one man draws out the wire, another straights it, a third cuts it, a fourth points it, a fifth grinds it at the top for receiving the head; to make the head requires three distinct operations; to put on is a peculiar business, to whiten the pins is another; it is even a trade in itself to put them into the paper...*

KEY IDEA

Division of labour
The division of labour is the process necessitating the subjugation of individuality, but allowing for the complex tasks of society to be achieved, through splitting up complex tasks into simpler ones, shared by several people. In this way, Smith sees much greater things can be achieved.

Now he suggests ten people could produce:

> *about twelve pounds of pins a day. There are in a pound upwards of four thousand pins of middling size. Those ten persons, therefore, could make upwards of forty-eight thousand pins a day. But if they had all wrought them separately ... they could certainly not each of them made twenty, perhaps not one pin a day.*

Smith then goes on to relate this advantage to:

* the accumulation of capital;

* the increase of employment; and

* the emergence of mechanisms to control the resulting tendency for wages to increase.

Also, the concentration on a particular task has a second benefit – the specialist develops better tools and methods.

A greater part of the machines made use of in those manufactures in which labour is most subdivided, were originally the inventions of common workmen, who being each of them employed in some very simple operation, naturally turned their thoughts towards finding out easier and readier methods of performing it. Whoever has been much accustomed to visit such manufacturers, must frequently have been shown very pretty machines, which were the inventions of such workmen, in order to facilitate and quicken their own particular part of the work.

The specializing encourages people to think of ways of improving their specific task, improvements otherwise obscured by the complexities of the whole process. Smith offers a rather feeble story to illustrate that industrial inventions are largely a fairly mundane process of refinement carried out by workers, rather than the grand inspiration of the pure 'inventor' as might be imagined.

In the first fire engines, a boy was constantly employed to open and shut alternately the communication between the boiler and the cylinder, according as the piston either ascended or descended. One of those boys, who loved to play with his companions, observed that, by tying a string from the handle of the valve, which opened this communication, to another part of the machine, the valve would open and shut without his assistance, and leave him at liberty to divert himself with his play-fellows. One of the greatest improvements that has been made upon this machine, since it was first invented, was in this manner the discovery of a boy who wanted to save his own labour.

SOCIAL COSTS OF THE DIVISION OF LABOUR

Smith sees the process of the division of labour as essentially *desirable*, in economic terms. In social terms, he has his doubts. . . People are all much of a muchness, although jobs make the man.

When the philosopher and the beggar, for example, came into the world, 'neither their parents nor their play-fellows could perceive any remarkable difference'. But pity the factory worker. He 'has no occasion to exert his understanding or to exercise his invention... He naturally loses, therefore the habit of such exertion, and generally becomes as stupid and ignorant as it is possible for a human creature to become...'. The factory hand, performing a monotonous simple task allotted to him by the logic of the division of labour, becomes equally monotonous and simple minded. The farm worker, on the other hand, remains much more 'a whole man', to Smith's eye.

The man who ploughs the ground with a team of oxen works with instruments of which the health, strength and temper are very different upon different occasions. The condition of the materials he works upon too is as variable as that of the instruments he works with, and both require to be managed with much judgement and discretion. The common ploughman, though generally regarded as the pattern of stupidity and ignorance, is seldom defective in his judgement and discretion. He is less accustomed, indeed, to social intercourse than the mechanick who lives in a town. His voice and language are more uncouth and more difficult to be understood by those who are not used to them. His understanding, however, being accustomed to consider a greater variety of objects, is generally much superior to that of the other, whose whole attention from morning till night is commonly occupied in performing one or two very simple operations.

Smith sees the state as having a responsibility to counter the *undesirable* effects of the division of labour through a programme of compulsory education, as well as (like Plato) through ensuring public entertainments are of an uplifting kind. His *laissez-faire* approach does not extend to education, where, for a 'very small expence the publick can facilitate, can encourage and can even impose upon almost the whole body of the people, the necessity of acquiring those most essential parts of education.'

It is not just the factory hands who need educating. The trade of merchant has a particularly invidious influence. 'He belongs to an order of men whose interest is never exactly the same with that of the publick, and who accordingly have, upon many occasions, both deceived and oppressed it.' Landlords likewise are rendered stupid by virtue of the indolence of their calling. Only the agricultural worker, challenged by a wider range of skills and tasks remains as nature intended, both independent and agile of mind.

However, the realization of the significance of the division of labour also leads to subtler considerations of the nature of capital and wealth itself. One is that the amount of specialization possible depends on certain factors. The most important is the size of the market. Improvements in communications and transport increase the effective size of the market, as do removal of obstacles such as tariffs. For this reason, the coastal or riverside towns spawned the first civilizations.

As Smith puts it in the 'Lectures on Jurisprudence':

When James the sixth of Scotland said of the county of Fife, of which the inland parts were at that time very ill while the sea coast was extremely well cultivated, that it was like a coarse woollen coat edged with gold lace, the same might still be said of the greater part of our North American colonies...

Then again prior to the division of labour, each worker produced only enough for their own needs. Smith supposes, under the division of labour, anyone who produces something necessarily must keep the bulk of the product for exchange purposes.

THE MONEY SYSTEM

To explain how the money system works, Smith begins by asserting that there are two kinds of price, a natural one and a market one. Regulations and taxes tend to make the market price higher than the natural one, and that is bad. Taxes distort the use of resources and interfere with the natural balance of the trades. (Hence that theme of Smith's, that Britain should become a free port, with no tariffs on goods going in or out.)

When these goods are sold, the money generated is used partly for consumption, and partly for buying tools and raw materials, say, for the next round of production. This money is the producer's 'capital', and it is also divided into two types. There is money that is spent on new machines or buildings. This is **fixed capital**. Then there is money paid out to the producers of the raw materials, or indeed in wages, this is **circulating capital**, which is what keeps the whole money system going – what Smith dubs 'the great wheel of circulation'.

Let's pause a moment. On an individual scale, the distinctions seem a bit arbitrary, but taking a society as a whole, the difference between fixed and circulating capital is more clear. Fixed capital is people with their natural energy, skills and training, their homes, roads and factories, the machines and tools and every considerable thing that goes into them in a modern economy. Circulating capital consists of money in its various forms (these days often just electronic digits on a computer) and all the goods that are not being used in some sense. For example, food in a shop waiting to be sold, or a pile of coal at a depot. Even the shop itself, if it is potentially transferable as a business between people, is also part of the circulating capital. Savings, too, are crucial for the system. In fact, Smith has as low opinion of those who enjoy their money rather than save it.

With regard to profusion, the principle, which prompts to expence, is the passion for present enjoyment; which, though sometimes violent and very difficult to be restrained, is in general only momentary and occasional. But the principle which prompts to save, is the desire of bettering our condition, a desire which, though generally calm and dispassionate, comes with us from the womb, and never leaves us till we go into the grave... In the whole interval which separates those two moments, there is scarce perhaps a single instant in which any man is so perfectly and completely satisfied with his situation, as to be without any wish of alteration or improvement, of any kind. An augmentation of fortune is the means by which the greater part of men propose and wish to better their condition. It is the means the most vulgar and the most obvious; and the most likely way of augmenting their fortune, is to save and accumulate...

Bankruptcy, on the other hand, is:

... perhaps the greatest and most humiliating calamity which can befall an innocent man. The greater part of men, therefore, are sufficiently careful to avoid it. Some, indeed, do not avoid it, as some do not the gallows ... [It is] the highest impertinence and presumption, therefore, in kings and ministers, to pretend to watch over the economy of private people; and to restrain their expence either by sumptuary laws, or by prohibiting the importation of foreign luxuries. They are always, and without any exception, the greatest spendthrifts in the society. Let them look well after their own expense, and they may safely trust private people with theirs.

Saving is the only virtuous way.

KEY PASSAGE: WASTE

... what is annually saved is as regularly consumed as what is annually spent, and nearly in the same time too, but it is consumed by a different set of people. That portion of his revenue which a rich man annually spends, is in most cases consumed by idle guests, and menial servants, who leave nothing behind them in return for their consumption. That portion which he annually saves, as for the sake of the profit it is immediately employed as a capital, is consumed in the same manner and nearly in the same time too, but by a different set of people, by labourers, manufacturers, and artificers, who re-produce, with a profit the value of their annual consumption.

---

o Key terms: Here, Smith the economist combines with Smith the moralist. Words like *revenue, consumption, profit* and of course *capital,* begin to take on a new hue.

In fact, the *Wealth of Nations* is Smith's pulpit for an attack on waste. Parsimony is the great virtue.

Whatever, therefore, we may imagine the real wealth and revenue of a country to consist in, whether in the value of the annual produce of its land and labour, as plain reason seems to dictate; or in the quantity of the precious metals which circulate within it, as vulgar prejudices suppose; in either view of the matter, every prodigal appears to be a publick enemy, and every frugal man a publick benefactor.

Warming to his theme, Vicar Smith adds:

The effects of misconduct are often the same as those of prodigality. Every injudicious and unsuccessful project in agriculture, mines, fisheries, trade, or manufactures, tends in the same manner to diminish the funds destined for the

maintenance of productive labour. In every such project, though the capital is consumed by productive hands only, yet, as by the injudicious manner in which they are employed, they do not reproduce the full value of their consumption, there must always be some diminution in what would otherwise have been the productive funds of the society...

It can seldom happen, indeed, that the circumstances of a great nation can be much affected either by the prodigality or misconduct of individuals; the profusion or imprudence of some being always more than compensated by the frugality and good conduct of others.

Not that Smith is against the generous impulse of hospitality, he hastens to add, at the end of the chapter.

Notes to Chapter 2

The discussion of human nature is from Book I of the *Wealth of Nations,* especially Chapters i and ii. The discussion of the hidden hand is in Book IV, Chapter ii.

The description of the effects of the division of labour is in Book I Chapter x, and the benevolence quotation can be found in Book I, Chapter ii.

The description of 'Parsimonious Man' is in Book II, Chapter iii.

3 Money

Here we examine how Smith considers:

* the origins of money;

* the question of true worth; and

* the different types of capital.

ORIGINS OF MONEY

Book II opens with some observations on 'the Nature, Accumulation, and Employment of Stock', as Smith terms money and its various manifestations.

> *In that rude state of society in which there is no division of labour, in which exchanges are seldom made, and in which every man provides every thing for himself, it is not necessary that any stock should be accumulated or stored up beforehand in order to carry on the business of the society. Every man endeavours to supply by his own industry his own occasional wants as they occur. When he is hungry, he goes to the forest to hunt; when his coat is worn out, he cloaths himself with the skin of the first large animal he kills: and when his hut begins to go to ruin, he repairs it, as well as he can, with the trees and the turf that are nearest it.*

So far, so unlikely. But Smith continues undaunted to make his point:

> ## KEY PASSAGE: INTER-DEPENDENCE
>
> *But when the division of labour has once been thoroughly introduced, the produce of a man's own labour can supply but a very small part of his occasional wants. The far greater part of them are supplied by the produce of other men's labour, which he purchases with the produce, or, what is the same thing, with the price of the produce of his own.*

Which is where money comes in.

That wealth consists in money, or in gold and silver, is a popular notion which naturally arises from the double function of money, as the instrument of commerce, and as the measure of value. In consequence of its being the instrument of commerce, when we have money we can more readily obtain whatever else we have occasion for, than by means of any other commodity. The great affair, we always find, is to get money.

When that is obtained, there is no difficulty in making any subsequent purchase. In consequence of its being the measure of value, we estimate that of all other commodities by the quantity of money which they will exchange for. We say of a rich man that he is worth a great deal, and of a poor man that he is worth very little money. A frugal man, or a man eager to be rich, is said to love money; and a careless, a generous, or a profuse man, is said to be indifferent about it. To grow rich is to get money; and wealth and money, in short, are, in common language, considered as in every respect.

Money is, in fact, 'the great wheel of circulation', and is altogether different from the goods which are circulated by means of it. The revenue of the society consists in these goods and not in the wheel itself, which circulates them. In calculating either the gross or the neat (nett) revenue of any society, we must always deduct the whole value of the money from their whole annual circulation of money and goods, 'of which not a single farthing can ever make any part of either'.

Originally, at least at some point, the wheel is made of silver or gold, but in due course it comes to be made of paper, which is 'much less costly and sometimes equally convenient'. Actually, precious metals are not even particularly good measures of wealth: 'Equal quantities of labour will at distant times be purchased more nearly with equal quantities of corn, the subsistence of the labourer, than with equal quantities of gold and silver, or perhaps of any other commodity.' That is to say, corn is a better measure of value than gold, a point reinforced, Smith says, by history. We should recall that in the sixteenth century: 'The discovery of the abundant mines of America reduced... the value of gold and sliver in Europe to about a third of what it had been before.'

MAGIC MONEY

Now a peculiar feature of money comes into play. A hundred thousand pounds of paper money can perform the same role as a hundred thousand pounds of golden money. However, the paper money may need to be backed, as it were, by a small fraction of the amount of gold, depending on the confidence of the public that the paper promises will be honoured. In this way, the total supply of 'circulating capital' can be increased without any additional labour.

The commerce and industry of the country, however, it must be acknowledged, though they may be somewhat augmented, cannot be altogether so secure when they are thus, as it were, suspended upon the Daedalian wings of paper money, as when they travel upon the solid ground of gold and silver.

Smith says this, despite his research into historic prices having clearly shown that the 'real value of every other commodity is finally measured and determined by the proportion which its average money price bears to the average money price of corn' (Book IV, Ch. v). But having thereby himself put corn on a special pedestal, Smith then tries to pull it down, decrying the public attitude to it as superstition.

The laws concerning corn may every where be compared to the laws concerning religion. The people feel themselves so much interested in what relates either to their subsistence in this life, or to their happiness in a life to come, that governments must yield to their prejudices and, in order to preserve the publick tranquillity, establish that system which they approve of.

Smith sees indeed what lurks behind the corn:

Labour alone, therefore, never varying in its own value, is alone the ultimate and real standard by which the value of all commodities can at all times and places be estimated and compared. It is their real price, money is their nominal price only.

If it usually costs twice the labour to kill a beaver as it does to kill a deer, says Smith, choosing an improbable example even in his day, 'one beaver should naturally exchange for or be worth two deer.' It is natural that what is usually the produce of two days' or two hours' labour would be worth double of what is usually the produce of one day's or one hour's labour. But this actually shows the limits of his theory – we need an element of what Marxists call 'use value' – and what 'use' is a dead beaver anyway?

Another consideration for Smith in calculating the basis for monetary exchange, is that 'the whole produce of labour does not always belong to the labourer'. He must in most cases share it with the owner of the stock which employs him.

As soon as the land of any country has all become private property, the landlords, like all other men, love to reap where they never sowed, and demand a rent even for the natural produce. The wind of the forest, the grass of the field, and all the natural fruits of the earth, which, when land was in common, cost the labourer only the trouble of gathering them, come even to him, to have an additional price fixed upon them.

In the price of corn, for example, 'one part pays the rent of the landlord, another pays the wages or maintenance of the labourers and labouring cattle employed in producing it, and the third pays the profit of the farmer.' In the price of flour or meal, 'we must add to the price of the corn, the profits of the miller, and the wages of the servants; in the price of the bread, the profits of the baker, and the wages of his servants'; and in the price of both, 'the labour of transporting the corn from the house of the farmer to that of the miller, and from that of the miller to that of the baker, together with the profits of those who advance the wages of that labour.'

Because commodities are normally exchanged for other commodities:

... it is more natural, therefore to estimate its exchangeable value by the quantity of some other commodity than by that of the labour which it can purchase... [and] when barter ceases, and money has become the common instrument of commerce, every particular commodity is more frequently exchanged for money than for any other commodity. The butcher seldom carries his beef or his mutton to the baker...

However, Smith continues:

... though equal quantities of labour are always of equal value of the labourer, yet to the person who employs him they appear sometimes to be of greater and sometimes of smaller value. His purchases them sometimes with a greater and sometimes with a smaller quantity of goods, and to him the price of labour seems to vary like that of all other things. It appears to him dear in the one case, and cheap in the other. In reality, however, it is the goods which are cheap in the one case and dear in the other.

THE IMPORTANCE OF CIRCULATING MONEY

However, the story of money is a bit more complicated than that. After all 'first man', so to speak, cannot purchase anything until he has something to purchase it with. In the absence of barter, that requires him to have not only already produced goods, through his labour, but to have sold them, too.

A stock of goods of different kinds, therefore, must be stored up somewhere sufficient to maintain him, and to supply him with the materials and tools of his work till such time, at least, as both these events can be brought about.

Book II, then, is an attempt to describe the nature of these goods – the 'stock' – both of individuals and of societies, as well as the nature of money, which is now seen only as 'a particular branch of the general stock of society'. Capital itself is a particularly useful form of stock which can be used either by its owner, or lent to others. After all, 'A man must be perfectly crazy, who, where there is tolerable security, does not employ all the stock which he commands, whether it be his own, or borrowed of other people...'.

The first distinction to be made is between fixed and circulating stock.

A stock of cloaths may last several years: a stock of furniture half a century or a century: but a stock of houses, well-built and properly taken care of, may last many centuries. Though the period of their consumption however is more distant, they are still as really a stock reserved for immediate consumption as either cloaths or household furniture.

In fact, of all the types of stock, that reserved for houses 'is the most slowly consumed'.

Some part of the capital of every 'master artificer' or manufacturer is, of necessity, fixed in the instruments of their trade. This part may be very small in some, and very great in others. A master tailor requires no other instruments but a parcel of needles. Those of the master shoemaker are a little, though but a very little, more expensive. The requirements of the weaver rise a good deal above those of the shoemaker. And the keeper of an inn or tavern, 'who is never master of his own house, and who is exposed to the brutality of every drunkard, exercises neither a very agreeable nor a very creditable business. But there is scarce a common trade in which a small stock yields so great a profit.' But in general, the far greater part of the capital of all 'master artificers', however, is circulated, either in the wages of their workmen, or in the price of their materials, and repaid with a profit by the price of the work.

FIXED CAPITAL

In some trades a much greater fixed capital is required. In a great iron-work, for example, 'the furnace for melting the ore, the forge, the slitt-mill, are instruments of trade which cannot be erected without a very great expense. In coal-works and mines of every kind, the machinery necessary both for drawing out the water and for other purposes, is frequently still more expensive.' And always the 'intention of the fixed capital is to increase the productive powers of labour, or to enable the same numbers of labourers to perform a greater quantity of work.'

Different occupations require very different proportions between the fixed and circulating capitals employed in them. Circulating capital consists of all the goods 'provisions, materials and finished work of all kinds', plus money. The capital of a merchant, for example, is altogether a circulating capital. He has occasion for no machines or instruments of trade, unless his shop, or warehouse, are considered as such.

The goods of the merchant yield him no revenue or profit till he sells them for money, and the money yields him as little till it is again exchanged for goods. His capital is continually going from him in one shape, and returning to him in another, and it is only by means of such circulation, or successive exchanges, that it can yield him any profit. Such capitals, therefore, may very properly he called circulating capitals.

Secondly, it [circulating capital] may be employed in the improvement of land, in the purchase of useful machines and instruments of trade, or in suchlike things as yield a revenue or profit without changing masters, or circulating any further. Such capitals, therefore, may very properly be called fixed capitals.

KEY PASSAGE: CIRCULATING CAPITAL

No fixed capital can yield any revenue but by means of circulating capital. The most useful machines and instruments of trade will produce nothing without the circulating capital which affords the materials they are employed upon, and the maintenance of the workmen who employ them. Land, however improved, will yield no revenue without a circulating capital, which maintains the labourers who cultivate and collect in the produce.

To 'maintain and augment the stock which may be reserved for immediate consumption', is the sole end and purpose both of the fixed and circulating capitals. It is this stock which feeds, clothes and lodges the people. 'Their riches or poverty depend upon the abundant or sparing supplies which these two capitals can afford to the stock reserved for immediate consumption.' However, the supply of the circulating capital itself must be continually replenished, from the agricultural, mining and fishing industries, or so Smith supposes. He has seen the consequences of neglecting this himself. 'The inhabitants of a large village, it has sometimes been observed, after having made considerable progress in manufactures, have become idle and poor; in consequence of a great lord's having taken up residence in their neighbourhood.' This goes to show that: 'Wherever capital predominates, industry prevails: wherever revenue: idleness.'

Not to assume, however, that hard work on its own is enough. 'Parsimony, and not industry, is the immediate source of the increase of capital... whatever industry might acquire, if parsimony did not save and store up, the capital would never be the greater.'

Dr Pangloss is mocked acerbically by Voltaire in his novel *Candide*, for his conviction – despite the ever-accumulating evidence to the contrary – that everything is for the best in all possible worlds. Similar serendipity is an indispensable element of Smith's analysis. But Smith is also following an older tradition, one that can be traced back to the Stoics of ancient Greece and Mesopotamia and indeed, before them, to eastern notions of harmony. The tendency of supply and demand to reach an equilibrium, and of the market price to reflect the underlying 'natural price' are central to this philosophy.

Smith is often demonized by those who aspire (at least) to be do-gooders, for advocating so powerfully laissez-faire economics (leaving things to sort themselves out without government interference) an advocacy that carries western governments before it even today. It is not so often recognized that this was because he himself certainly believed that if this were done the outcome would be not just acceptable, but the best possible for everyone. 'What encourages the progress of population and improvement, encourages that of real wealth and greatness' he writes towards the end of the *Wealth of Nations*. Free trade encourages countries to specialize in what they are good at, and forces them to give up doing what they are not. This results in more goods being produced in total (because they are produced more efficiently). At this stage of our analysis, we must look at Smith's persuasive case for 'free trade', and this will the theme of the next chapter.

Notes to Chapter 3

Smith's discussion of the origins and role of money take place in Book I, Chapters v and vi, and Book II, Chapter ii. He returns to the subject of pricing in Book IV, Chapter i where he also looks in more detail at corn prices, in Chapter v.

The discussion of the nature of circulating and fixed capitals in centred on Book II, Chapters i and ii, as well as at the end of Book I and the beginning of Book III.

4 Free Trade and Free Education

Now we examine how, in Books IV and VII, Smith describes the role and advantages of free trade (and makes what for him, is very nearly a humorous obervation).

THE ADVANTAGES OF FREE TRADE

By the second chapter of Book IV, of *Wealth of Nations* Smith's mind has turned to wine making.

The natural advantages which one country has over another in producing particular commodities are sometimes so great, that it is acknowledged by all the world to be in vain to struggle with them. By means of glasses, hotbeds, and hotwalls, very good grapes can be raised in Scotland, and very good wine too can be made of them at about thirty times the expense for which at least equally good can be brought from foreign countries. Would it be a reasonable law to prohibit the importation of all foreign wines, merely to encourage the making of claret and burgundy in Scotland?

But it is a digression with a serious purpose. Smith leaves us in no doubt of his own opinion.

KEY PASSAGE: TRADING SPECIALIZATION

But if there would be a manifest absurdity in turning towards any employment, thirty times more of the capital and industry of the country, than would be necessary to purchase from foreign countries an equal quantity of the commodities wanted, there must be an absurdity, though not altogether so glaring, yet exactly of the same kind, in turning towards any such employment a thirtieth, or even a three hundredth part more of either. Whether the advantages which one country has over another, be natural or acquired is of no consequence.

o *the advantages* of free trade: This theory of mutual advantage is the distinctive thread that runs through the *Wealth of Nations* and made Smith's name.

He compares free trade with the kind of everyday trading occasioned by the division of labour and thus practised by an individual family in the country. And this is only part of a wider theory of the benefits of deregulation and *laissez-faire*. For Smith, it is a policy that serves the interests of all, rich and poor alike.

THE ROLE OF THE STATE

Smith's free trade beliefs follow from consideration of the two then rival economic systems: the mercantile and the physiocratic. The mercantile system is flawed, as we saw earlier, simply because it measures wealth in terms of money. Smith believes that true wealth is in manufactured goods. As for the physiocrats, their mistake is less deplorable but still important. Their 'capital error' is to regard agriculture as the only source of wealth, and to leave the rest of the economy as unproductive – merely changing the wealth from one form to another. But at least the physiocrats realized that wealth ultimately consisted in the 'consumable', rather than the unconsumable (that is, money) and furthermore, Smith adds, at least they recognized that 'perfect liberty' was the best way to maximize 'this annual reproduction'.

Actually, unlike Quesnay, Smith accepted that even with imperfect governments interfering to some extent with liberty, a certain amount of prosperity is still possible. Indeed, any of 'those exertions of the natural liberty' which might endanger the security of the whole society could and indeed should be regulated out of existence.

Such an exception can be made in the name of 'defence', which actually was the original justification for the Navigation Acts. Then again, a tariff can be justified if the equivalent domestic product is already taxed – this is only to even up a skewed market. It is a recognition that to expect 'indeed, that the freedom of trade would ever be entirely restored in Great Britain, is as absurd as to expect an Oceania or Utopia should ever be established in it.'

Smith allows the State three, carefully delineated jobs.

* Defence (as already mentioned) is the State's primary role. The first duty of the sovereign is 'that of protecting the society from the violence and invasion of other independent societies'. This can be done 'only by military force'. 'The art of war,' Smith continues somewhat unexpectedly, 'is certainly the noblest of all arts', and it is appropriate that it should be allocated to specialists, to 'become the sole or principal occupation of a particular class of citizens'.

* The administration of justice is the second duty of sovereign. This second task is 'the duty of protecting, so far as possible, every member of the society from the injustice or oppression of every other member of it.'

> *Among nations of hunters, as there is scarce any property or at least none that exceeds the value of two or three days labour; so there is seldom any established magistrate or any regular administration of justice. Men who have no property can injure one another only in their persons or reputations. But where one man kills, wounds, beats or defames another, though he to whom injury is done suffers, he who does it receives no benefit. It is otherwise with injuries to property ... Envy, malice or resentment are the only passions which can prompt one man to injure another in his person or reputation. But the greater part of men are not very frequently under the influence of these passions, and the very worst men are so only occasionally ... But avarice and ambition in the rich, in the poor the hatred of labour and the love of present ease and enjoyment, are the passions which*

promote to invade property, passions much more steady in their operation, and much more universal in their influence.

As property accumulates, so does inequality, Smith adds. 'The affluence of the rich excites the indignation of the poor, who are often both driven by want and prompted by envy, to invade his possessions.' The rich man, is 'surrounded at all times by unknown enemies, whom, though he never provoked, he can never appease'. Only the might of the law can protect him. Thus it is that property necessitates and occasions the development of civil government. And with it new forms of 'subordination'. Added to strength, beauty, agility, wisdom and so on, and to age, 'is the superiority of riches and fortune'. As a result of inheritance, comes the superiority of birth. 'Birth and fortune are evidently the two circumstances which principally set one man above another.'

✳ The carrying out of public works makes up the third role. In particular, any such that private enterprise would be inadequate to perform.

This third task, however, goes beyond the first two in kind, as it gives the State a positive, proactive role. Smith sees public works as capable of providing the 'infrastructure', roads, canals, ports, railways etc., for a successfully functioning private economy, but he also sees the State as providing certain 'social' services, the most important of which is providing all citizens with a basic education. So, the State is left with a minimal role, not only in defence and law and order, but any of those services that commerce will not bother with – such as building sewers or bridges and providing elementary schools. 'It does seem necessary that the expence of those publick works should be defrayed from that publick revenue', he writes. Then there is the Mint for making the currency itself, and indeed the lights to facilitate travel.

Smith believes that in all cases the advantages of keeping the relationship immediate and direct between those who charge and those who pay, is primary; and this means not all enterprises are best in private hands – Smith offers transport as an example. A privately owned road can be profitable even when poorly looked after by the unscrupulous, so it is better for the State to provide them and maintain higher standards although the State may be unreliable in its own way.

> *Were the streets of London to be lighted and paved at the expence [sic] of the treasury, is there any probability that they would be so well lighted and paved as they are at present, or even at so small an expence?'*

The expense besides,

> *'instead of being raised by a local tax upon the inhabitants of each particular street parish or district in London, would , in this case, be defrayed out of the general revenue of the State, and would consequently be raised by a tax upon all the inhabitants of the kingdom, of whom the greater part derive no sort of benefit from the lighting and paving of the streets of London.*

Conversely, canals must be maintained, otherwise the private owner can make no money out of them, so they can be left in private hands. As far as education goes, Smith recommends the practice current then in Scotland (and which he himself had experienced) of making teachers and professors depend upon the satisfaction of their classes for their wages. Where this link is broken, remember Smith warns, slackness obtains (as at Oxford). Whether Smith would consider it important to consider the possibility that every inhabitant of a modern country may benefit from general lighting and paving of streets, with a wider interest than just their home town, is not clear. Nonetheless, it must remain true that those who live in London have a stronger reason to guard against inadequate provision of a service and to protest at excessive charges for it.

However, as Smith goes on to say, the abuses 'which sometimes creep in to the local and provincial administration of a local and provincial revenue, how enormous soever they appear, are in reality, however almost always very trifling, in comparison with those which commonly take place in the administration and expenditure of the revenue of a great empire.' Put another way, take powers away from the centre and you limit the scale of that institution's abuses.

THE TEMPORARY MONOPOLY

Smith actually even allows a brief monopoly for the purposes of setting up a new trade route, or for 'hazarding a dangerous and expensive experiment, of which the publick is afterwards to reap the benefit'. But it must be strictly a temporary monopoly, similar to that justified by invention for the creator of a new machine, or an author of a new book. Total monopoly penalizes people in two ways, both in raising prices higher than they would be if the goods were traded freely and, by being excluded from the trade as active participants. 'It is merely to enable the company to support the negligence, profusion, and malversation of their own servants, whose disorderly conduct seldom allows the dividend of the company to exceed the ordinary rate of profit in trades which are ordinarily free, and very frequently it makes it fall even a good deal short of that rate.' Such debates are by no means redundant, the extent of trade liberalization through agencies such as the World Trade Organisation are paralleled by the ever accumulating monopoly powers of transnational giants, or the use of patents to claim the exclusive trading rights. These are private companies whose turnover may exceed those of the countries they are trading in.

EDUCATION

What is the role of the State in 'Institutions for the Education of Youth'? Smith is concerned that State assistance should not weaken the relationship between teaching quality and teaching remuneration. Endowments and other such State assistance, he considers 'necessarily' diminish 'the necessity of application in the teachers. Their subsistence, so far as it arises from their salaries, is evidently derived from a fund altogether independent of their success and reputation in their particular profession.' A similar problem arises with charitable support for students which points them at a particular institution.

There are no public institutions for the education of women, Smith perhaps rather smugly notes, 'and there is accordingly nothing useless, absurd or fantastical in the common course of their education'. Every thing they learn is directed towards becoming 'mistresses of a family, and to behave properly when they have become such'. On the other hand, 'it seldom happens that a man, in any part of his life, derives any conveniency or advantage from some of the most laborious and troublesome parts of education.'

Education is made increasingly vital by the development of modern industry, and the effects of the division of labour. Smith begins in a typically pedestrian way:

The man whose whole life is spent in performing a few simple operations, of which the effects too are, perhaps, always the same, or every nearly the same, has no occasion to exert his understanding, or to exercise his invention in finding out expedients for removing difficulties which never occur. He naturally loses, therefore the habit of such exertion and becomes as stupid and ignorant as it is possible for a human creature to become. The torpor of his mind renders him, not only incapable of relishing or bearing a part in any rational conversation, but of conceiving any generous, noble, or tender sentiment, and consequently of forming any just judgement concerning many even of the ordinary duties of private life. Of the great and extensive interests of his country, he is altogether incapable of judging; and unless very particular pains have

been taken to render him otherwise, he is equally incapable
of defending his country in war. The uniformity of his
stationary life naturally corrupts the courage of his mind,
and makes him regard with abhorrence the irregular,
uncertain and adventurous life of a soldier.

Just as Rousseau supposed with his description of the 'Noble Savage',
'It corrupts even the strength of his body, and renders him incapable
of exerting his strength with vigour and perseverance...'.

Education instead should be relevant and efficient. The '3Rs' are
prescribed by Smith. He calls them 'the most essential parts of
education', that is to 'read, write and account'.

The publick can facilitate this acquisition by establishing in
every parish or district a little school, where children may
be taught for a reward so moderate that even a common
labourer can afford it; the master being partly, but not
wholly paid by the publick; because if he was wholly or even
principally paid by it, he would soon learn to neglect his
business.

However, this approach, of always retaining a 'market' element in
public service, has largely been lost – schools are completely free, or
(ostensibly) completely paid for. Perhaps surprisingly, Smith goes on
to advocate a compulsory exam of sorts to be used as a way of
imposing minimum literacy on the population, and without
passing, people would be barred from 'any trade either in a village or
town corporate'.

By forcibly dispelling 'the gross ignorance and stupidity which, in a
civilized society, seem so frequently to benumb the understandings
of all the inferior ranks of people', society gains a great benefit. Not
just in terms of suppressing criminal behaviour, Smith supposes, but
because an 'instructed and intelligent people besides are always more
decent and orderly than an ignorant and stupid one.'

LIBERTY AND THE MARKET

A particular problem arose for Smith to address – that of religious sectarianism. Smith has two remedies, the first 'the study of science and philosophy'. This should be made 'universal amongst all people of middling or more than middling rank and fortune', through a similar sort of test, although more difficult, to that recommended for the workers in literacy and so on. The State would confine itself to making such philosophizing compulsory, as if the State imposed upon this order of men the necessity of learning, it would have no occasion to give itself any trouble about providing them with proper teachers. And finally, as it were, Smith suggests (boldly) that 'entire liberty' should be given to those who 'for their own interest, without scandal or indecency, … amuse and divert the people by painting, poetry, musick and dancing; by all sorts of dramatic representations and exhibitions.' In this way, 'that melancholy and gloomy humour which is almost always the nurse of popular superstition and enthusiasm' would be dissipated.

That said, everything else can be left to the market. This is because everyone, Smith claims, 'labours to render the annual revenue of the society as great as he can'. They may generally, indeed, neither intend to promote the public interest, nor know how much they are doing so, but promote it they do. The citizen, by pursuing his own interest, 'frequently promotes that of the society more effectually than when he really intends to promote it', unlike public bodies ostensibly charged with that task. By contrast, 'Public services are never better performed than where their reward comes only in consequence of their being performed, and is proportioned to the diligence employed in performing them.' In fact, Smith says, 'I have never known much good done by those who affected to trade for the publick good. It is an affectation, indeed not very common amongst merchants, and very few words need be employed in dissuading them from it.'

It is lucky and fortunate indeed that the public good can largely look after itself.

KEY PASSAGE: NON-INTERFERENCE

What is the species of domestick industry which his capital can employ, and of which the produce is likely to be of the greatest value, every individual, it is evident, can, in his local situation, judge much better than any statesman or lawgiver can do for him. The statesman who should attempt to direct private people in what manner they ought to employ their capitals, would not only load himself with a most unnecessary attention, but assume an authority which could safely be trusted, not only to no single person, but to no council or senate whatever, and which would nowhere be so dangerous as in the hands of a man who had folly and presumption enough to fancy himself fit to exercise it.

In the *Moral Sentiments*, Smith had put it like this:

The rich consume little more than the poor, and in spite of their natural selfishness and capacity, though they mean only their own conveniency, though the sole end which they propose from the labours of all the thousands whom they employ, be the gratification of their own vain and insatiable desires, they divide with the poor the produce of all their improvements, they are led by an invisible hand to make nearly the same distribution of the necessaries of life, which would have been made, had the earth been divided into equal portions among all its inhabitants...

To some, this earlier sentiment exposes Smith's social myopia, not to say his foolishness. But taken in more holistic 'macro-economic' terms, the 'invisible hand' does indeed spread the wealth around, as he says, necessarily. Smith was a scientist of society, he made his observations with as honest and open a mind as any mere human could be expected to and he was struck by the way in which the market does seem to work as a self-regulating machine, balancing supply and demand with changes in prices. And it is only having observed and found this natural harmony, that Smith comes to be so passionate in this opposition to those foolish interventions in the economy which governments, being made up of humans, are always inclined to make. The most foolish interferences, to Smith's mind, were the restrictions on competition, along with obstacles to labour mobility and those on free trade.

By way of illustration, Smith mentions specifically restrictive practices such as the demands of trades for apprentices to serve their apprenticeships before they could practise, and the Poor Law – notably the restriction of charity to people living in the same parish that they were born in. He writes, for example: 'To remove a man who has committed no misdemeanour from the parish where he chooses to reside, is an evident violation of natural liberty and justice.'

Take the first of these 'interferences'. Since Smith believes all groups in industrial society are interdependent: owners depend on workers for their income; workers depend on bosses for the opportunities to profit from their labour, it is as bad for bosses to 'buck the market' as anyone else.

When masters combine together in order to reduce the wages of their workmen, they commonly enter into a private bond of agreement, not to give more than a certain wage under a certain penalty. Were the workmen to enter into a contrary combination of the same kind, not to accept of a certain wage under a certain penalty, the law would punish them very severely; and if it dealt impartially, it would treat the masters in the same manner.

Smith demands in a similar vein, the abolition of regulations and for the government to 'break down the exclusive privileges of corporations, and repeal the statutes of apprenticeship, both of which are real encroachments upon natural liberty, and add to these the repeal of the law of settlement, so that a poor workman, when thrown out of employment either in one trade or in one place, may seek for it in another trade or in another place, 'without the fear... of a prosecution.' But Smith reserves his main fire for the Navigation Acts, which occasions his wine-making theme, and a wider discussion of free trade.

What is prudence in the conduct of every private family, can scarce be folly in that of a great kingdom. If a foreign country can supply us with a commodity cheaper than we ourselves can make it, better buy it off them with some part of the produce of our own industry, employed in a way in which we have some advantage. The general industry of the country, being always in proportion to the capital which employs it, will not thereby be diminished, no more than that of the above mentioned artificers; but only left to find out the way in which it can be employed with the greatest advantage. It is certainly not employed to the greatest advantage, when it is thus directed towards an object which it can buy cheaper than it can make.

Whenever an attempt is made to do so, the industry of the country is 'turned away from a more, to a less advantageous employment', and the 'exchangeable value of its annual produce, instead of being increased, according to the intention of the lawgiver, must necessarily be diminished by every such regulation.' In fact:

No regulation of commerce can increase the quantity of industry in any society beyond what its capital can maintain. It can only divert a part of it into a direction which it might not otherwise have gone, and it is by no means certain that this artificial distinction is likely to be more advantageous to the society than that into which it would have gone of its own accord.

TRAVEL AND THE MARKET

Smith notes that the division of labour is limited by the size of the available market. In a village, the specialization is less, in a town it is more. In the town carpentry, joinery, cabinet-making, wood-carving are separate occupations of different skilled people, in the village one person will do all of them.

In the lone houses and very small villages which are scattered about in so desert a country as the lands of Scotland, every farmer must be butcher, baker and brewer for his own family... A country carpenter deals in every sort of work that is made of wood... not only a carpenter, but a joiner, a cabinet maker, and even a carver in wood, as well as a wheelwright, a plough-wright, a cart and wagon-maker.

(Bk I, Ch. iii)

As by means of water-carriage a more extensive market is opened to every sort of industry than what land-carriage alone can afford it, so it is upon the sea-coast, and along the banks of navigable rivers, that industry of every kind naturally begins to subdivide and improve itself...

A broad-wheeled wagon, attended by two men, and drawn by eight horses, in about six weeks' time carries and brings back between London and Edinburgh near four ton weight of goods. In about the same time a ship navigated by six or eight men, and sailing between the ports of London and Leith, frequently carries and brings back two hundred ton weight of goods... [equivalent to] fifty broad-wheeled wagons, attended by a hundred men, and drawn by four hundred horses.

Without boats, what goods could bear the expense of carriage between London and Calcutta? Egypt was the

> *first country to improve itself and it extends nowhere*
> *above a few miles from the Nile. Neither the ancient*
> *Egyptians, the Indians, nor the Chinese encouraged*
> *foreign commerce, but seem all to have derived their great*
> *opulence from this inland-navigation.* (Bk I, Ch. iii)

We might add that the same applies on a regional level too. For example, within a state, improving road links may remove physical obstacles to trade with the effect of making a region's special wine or wooly jumpers worth transporting to the rest of the country. However, as poorer regions also know, the reverse is also true: large efficient companies outside the region can move in and displace even the last few small cottage industries of the local communities. The overall gains may eventually be at the clear expense of the small region.

SMITH'S SCOTTISH SETTING

Ironically, in Smith's days, Glasgow was built upon the wealth of the carrying trade, that trade which the *Wealth of Nations* derides as the 'least productive' way of using stock, and worse still, a trade based on mercantile restrictions to the New World. Many of Smith's recommendations, if implemented, would have destroyed the livelihoods of those he met and hobnobbed with in the city. Nonetheless:

> *To give the monopoly of the home-market to the produce of*
> *domestick industry, in any particular art or manufacture, is*
> *in some measure to direct private people in what manner*
> *they ought to employ their capitals, and must, in almost all*
> *cases, be either a useless or a hurtful regulation. If the*
> *produce of domestick can be brought there as cheap as that*
> *of foreign industry, the regulation is evidently useless. If it*
> *cannot, it must generally be hurtful. It is the maxim of*
> *every prudent master of a family, never to attempt to make*

at home what it will cost him more to make than to buy. The taylor does not attempt to make his own shoes, but buys them of the shoemaker. The shoemaker does not attempt to make his own cloaths, but employs a taylor. The farmer attempts to make neither the one nor the other, but employs those different artificers. All of them find it for their interest to employ their whole industry in a way in which they have some advantage over their neighbours, and to purchase with a part of its produce, or what is the same thing, with the price of a part of it, whatever else they have occasion for.

MONOPOLY

That it was the spirit of monopoly which originally both invented and propagated this doctrine, cannot be doubted; and they who first taught it were by no means such fools as they who believed it. In every country it always is and must be the interest of the great body of the people to buy whatever they want of those who sell it cheapest. The proposition is so very manifest, that it seems ridiculous to take any pains to prove it; nor could it ever have been called in question, had not the interested sophistry of merchants and manufacturers confounded the common sense of mankind. Their interest is, in this respect, directly opposite to that of the great body of the people. As it is the interest of the freemen of a corporation to hinder the rest of the inhabitants from employing any workmen but themselves, so it is the interest of the merchants and manufacturers of every country to secure to themselves the monopoly of the home market. Hence in Great Britain, and in most other countries, the extraordinary duties upon almost all goods imported by alien merchants. Hence the high duties and prohibitions upon all those foreign manufactures which can come into competition with our own. Hence too the extraordinary restraints upon the importation of almost all sorts of goods from those countries with which the balance of trade is supposed to be disadvantageous; that is, from those against whom national animosity happens to be most violently inflamed.

The wealth of a neighbouring nation, however, though dangerous in war and politicks, is certainly advantageous in trade. In a state of hostility it may enable our enemies to maintain fleets and armies superior to our own; but in a state of peace and commerce it must likewise enable them to exchange with us to a greater value, and to afford a better market, either for the immediate produce of our own industry, or for whatever is purchased with that produce. As a rich man is likely to be a better customer to the industrious people in his neighbourhood, than a poor, so is likewise a rich nation. A rich man, indeed, who is himself a manufacturer, is a very dangerous neighbour to all those who deal in the same way. All the rest of the neighbourhood, however, by far the greatest number, profit by the good market which his expense affords them. They even profit by his under-selling the poorer workmen who deal in the same way with him. The manufacturers of a rich nation, in the same manner, may no doubt be very dangerous rivals to those of their neighbours. This very competition, however, is advantageous to the great body of the people, who profit greatly besides by the good market which the great expense of such a nation affords them in every other way. Private people who want to make a fortune, never think of retiring to the remote and poor provinces of the country, but resort either to the capital or to some of the great commercial towns. They know, that, where little wealth circulates, there is little to be got, but that where a great deal is in motion, some share of it may fall to them.

The same maxims which would in this manner direct the common sense of one, or ten, or twenty individuals, should regulate the judgement of one, or ten, or twenty millions, and should make a whole nation regard the riches of its neighbours, as a probable cause and occasion for itself to acquire riches. A nation that would enrich itself by foreign trade is certainly most likely to do so when its neighbours are all rich, industrious, and commercial nations. A great nation surrounded on all sides by wandering savages and poor barbarians might, no doubt, acquire riches by the cultivation of its own lands, and by its own interior commerce, but not by foreign trade. It seems to have been in this manner that the ancient Egyptians and the modern Chinese acquired their great wealth. The ancient Egyptians, it is said, neglected foreign commerce, and the modern Chinese, it is known, hold it in the utmost contempt, and scarce deign to afford it the decent protection of the laws. The modern maxims of foreign commerce, by aiming at the impoverishment of all our neighbours, so far as they are capable of producing their intended effect, tend to render that very commerce insignificant and contemptible.

(Bk IV; Ch. iii)

Thanks to its gross interference in trade, 'Great Britain resembles one of those unwholesome bodies in which some of the vital parts are overgrown, and which, upon that account, are liable to many dangerous disorders...'.

Due to the fact that, in the mercantile system, economics had been turned upside down, and the interest of the consumer 'almost constantly sacrificed to that of the producer', it seemed evident to Smith that government policy took 'production, not consumption, as 'the ultimate end and object of all industry and commerce'. But ultimately, consumption is the sole end and purpose of all production, and it follows that 'the interest of the producer ought to be attended to, only so far as it may be necessary for promoting that of the consumer.' Smith says his maxim is so perfectly self-evident, that it would be absurd to attempt to prove it. It is altogether and only for the benefit of the producer, that the consumer is obliged to pay 'that enhancement of price' which monopoly occasions ...

... in the system of laws which has been established for the management of our American and West Indian colonies, the interest of the home-consumer has been sacrificed to that of the producer with a more extravagant profusion than in all our other commercial regulations. A great empire has been established for the sole purpose of raising up a nation of customers who should be obliged to buy from the shops of our different producers, all the goods with which these could supply them. For the sake of that little enhancement of price which this monopoly might afford our producers, the home-consumers have been burdened with the whole expense of maintaining and defending that empire. For this purpose, and for this purpose only, in the two last wars, more than two hundred millions have been spent, and a new debt of more than a hundred and seventy millions has been contracted over and above all that had been expended for the same purpose in former wars. The interest of this debt

alone is not only greater than the whole extraordinary profit, which, it ever could be pretended, was made by the monopoly of the colony trade, but than the whole value of that trade or than the whole value of the goods, which at an average have been annually exported to the colonies.

THE OBSTACLES TO FREE TRADE

Smith concludes, as we have seen, that to expect freedom of trade to be entirely restored, is as absurd as to expect that an Oceania or Utopia should be established, an absurdity due to the fact that 'not only the prejudices of the publick, but what is much more unconquerable, the private interests of many individuals, irresistibly oppose it.' This is practical politics. The transition from protectionism to free trade would entail hardship. But Smith thinks this is not an insurmountable obstacle.

The undertaker of a great manufacture who, by the home markets being suddenly laid open to the competition of foreigners, should be obliged to abandon his trade, would no doubt suffer very considerably… equitable regard, therefore to his interest requires that changes of this kind should never be introduced suddenly, but slowly, gradually, and after a very long warning.

The bigger problem is the lies of the businessmen.

… nations have been taught that their interest consisted in beggaring all their neighbours. Each nation has been made to look with an invidious eye upon the prosperity of all the nations with which it trades, and to consider their gain as its own loss. Commerce, which ought naturally to be, among nations, as among individuals, a bond of union and friendship, has become the most fertile source of discord and animosity. The capricious ambition of kings and ministers has not, during the present and the preceding century, been more fatal to the repose of Europe, than the impertinent

jealousy of merchants and manufacturers. The silence and injustice of the rulers of mankind is an ancient ill, for which, I am afraid, the nature of human affairs can scarce admit of a remedy. But the mean rapacity, the monopolising spirit of merchants and manufacturers, who neither are, nor ought to be the rulers of mankind, though it cannot perhaps be corrected, may very easily be prevented from disturbing the tranquillity of any body but themselves.

Smith concludes Book IV with an appeal for change:

It cannot be very difficult to determine who have been the contrivers of this whole mercantile system; not the consumers, we may believe, whose interest has been entirely neglected; but the producers whose interest has been so carefully attended to; and among this latter class our merchants and manufacturers have been by far the principal architects. In the mercantile regulations, which have been taken notice of in this chapter, the interest of our manufacturers has been most peculiarly attended to; and the interest, not so much of the consumers, as that of some other sets of producers, has been sacrificed to it.

Notes to Chapter 4

The absurd wine makers, along with the greedy corporations and the diminishing industries, are to be found in Book IV, Chapter ii. By Chapter vii of the same book, Great Britain is seen in its diseased state. The quotations from monopolies are from Book IV, Chapters iii and viii, and the description of the journeys of the broad-wheeled wagons and water carriages returns us to Book I, Chapter iii.

5 More Money

In this chapter, we follow Smith back to the counting house to examine the nature of money in more detail.

Smith has an indefatigable interest in the detail of the beginnings of money. The story starts with the exchange of goods can be carried out by barter – the butcher stockpiles some beef, the baker some loaves, and so on, but as there may be a baker who does not eat beef, or other practical shortcomings of the system, this soon gives way to exchange of goods by reference to one particular commodity. This may be gold or silver (or salt, which gave us the word 'salary'), but eventually leads to money itself. Smith describes at length (one of the most popular parts of the book) the transition to coinage, a process driven by the two related problems of how to stop people from adulterating the metals, or from filing small bits off all to make a little extra margin for themselves. Kings and Royal Mints were past masters at this, of course, with Roman silver coins, in the dying days of the Republic, worth just one twenty-fourth of what they had started out as. Smith, ever frugal himself, indignantly condemns 'the avarice and injustice of princes and sovereign states', who 'by abusing the confidence of their subjects', by degrees reduce the quantity of metal which had been originally contained in their coins.

That wealth consists in money, or in gold and silver, is a popular notion which naturally arises from the double function of money, as the instrument of commerce, and as the measure of value. In consequence of its being the instrument of commerce, when we have money we can more readily obtain whatever else we have occasion for, than by means of any other commodity. The great affair, we always find, is to get money.

REAL AND NOMINAL VALUES

In consequence of money being the measure of value, Smith explains that we estimate the worth of all other commodities 'by the quantity of money which they will exchange for: we say of a rich man that he is worth a great deal, and of a poor man that he is worth very little money. A frugal man, or a man eager to be rich, is said to love money; and a careless, a generous, or a profuse man, is said to be indifferent about it. To grow rich is to get money; and wealth and money, in short, are, in common language, considered as in every respect.'

However, if the value of the coin used to depend on the amount of silver in it – what gave the silver its value of our coin anyway? As we saw earlier, Smith says that the 'real price of every thing, what every thing really costs... is the toil and trouble of acquiring it.'

Or, in Smith's terms, 'Labour, therefore, is the real measure of the exchangeable value of commodities.'

Stepping aside from Smith, for a moment, for comparison, in Volume I of *Capital*, Marx says that: 'The value of any commodity, such as linen, is expressed in terms of numberless other elements of the world of commodities'. The usefulness of a thing gives it a [wait for it] use value. But this usefulness is conditioned by the 'physical properties of the commodity and has no existence apart from the latter'. Gold or money are what Marx calls the 'general form'.

> **KEY DEFINITION: PRICES**
>
> Prices are essentially measures of the amount of labour needed to make the commodity.

Meanwhile, rents paid in corn, Smith continues, after long perusal of corn market records, have always held their value far better than rents paid in anything else. 'From century to century, corn is the better measure because, from century to century, equal quantities of corn will command the same quantity of labour more nearly than equal quantities of silver.'

Now, on one level, this is obviously not true. (Ask an artist – or even an author!) But let Smith have his say. He admits it is more complicated than that. It is the 'nominal value' of goods that determines whether trade is profitable – so, for example, tea in China is cheap, and worth the while of the European importer purchasing. It is therefore nominal values that regulate 'almost the whole business of common life in which price is concerned – we cannot wonder that it should have been so much more attended to than the real price.'

Smith considers there to be a 'real' value for everything, and a 'nominal' value, which is its market valuation, its price. This real or 'natural' price is what Alfred Marshall later called the long-period price, around which a commodity gravitates, or as Smith says, 'The natural price, therefore, is as it were, the central price, to which the prices of all commodities are continually gravitating.'

When goods are sold at 'what is sufficient to pay the rent of the land, the wages of the labour, and the profits of the stock employed in raising, preparing and bringing it to market, according to their natural rates, the commodity is then sold for what may be called its natural price.'

This market price, on the other hand, is set by the happenstance of the supply as affected by the demand. Although it is not just any sort of demand, of course. 'A poor man may be said in some sense to have a demand for a coach and six, he might like to have it, but his demand is not an effectual demand, as the commodity can never be brought to market

KEY DEFINITION: NATURAL PRICES

The *natural price* of a product, according to Smith, is 'neither more nor less than what is sufficient to pay the rent of the land, the wages of the labourer, and the profits of the stock.'

MARKET PRICE

The actual price 'at which any commodity is commonly sold is called its market price'.

in order to satisfy it.' On the other hand, to dust off one of Smith's favourite examples, 'a publick mourning' raises the price of black cloth – demand is high, the price rises and more of the goods are produced. As more of the goods are produced, prices drop, and the incentive for the producer disappears, reducing supplies and increasing prices again.

o It is the nominal value that drives the marketplace.

The price someone is prepared to pay is determined by several factors. There is the psychological factor of how much they want it. There is the practical consideration of the manufacturer of how much they have had to spend already to produce the goods. This will include the wages of the workers, the share due to the people who have provided the investment in the machinery and premises for the manufacture, the rent of any equipment or land, and the cost of the raw materials. Smith distinguishes the types of cost because they have different effects. The workers require recompense simply for their time and effort, which he considers to be fairly straightforward.

Labour alone, never varying in its own value, is alone the ultimate and real standard by which the value of all commodities can at all times and places be estimated and compared. It is their real price; money is their nominal price only.

However, the labour of the manufacturer 'fixes and realises itself in some particular subject or vendible [saleable] commodity, which lasts for some time at least after that labour is past. It is, as it were, a certain quantity of labour stocked and sorted up to be employed, if necessary, upon some other occasion.'

Various examples are offered.

❋ There is the simple case of fish. Those caught from the sea involve only the labour and capital costs, those caught from rivers will also include a 'rent' charge, to the owner of the fishing rights.

❋ Then again, 'in some parts of Scotland a few poor people make a trade of gathering, along the sea-shore, those little variegated stones commonly known by the name of "Scotch Pebbles".' This is another simple form of production.

❋ Then there is the more sophisticated case of the factory. The owner of the factory requires a return on the investment, which varies with the amount of capital invested. This is because this capital could have been simply put in a bank (where the manager could then lend it to others for a small fee), and left to grow by compound interest.

Profit and interest are basically the same sort of thing – return on capital. Rent, Smith sees as different. The profit of the farmer or factory owner is not like a wage for managing – if it were, it must vary with the amount of time and bother involved. Instead, it varies with the amount of capital involved – whether it requires a lot of land. For farmers and factory owners, unlike mere rentiers, there is risk involved. But rent may simply be profit, a charge imposed without any original investment, and we might argue with Smith that because any asset that can be rented can probably be sold, too, the distinction seems to disappear.

Smith does recognize that the relationship of wages, profit and rent is a complex process, and that this is much more than just the interplay of supply and demand. His particular interest is in how money paid of commodities is distributed amongst the three groups that correspond to the original price, that is to say, the workers and labour part, the capitalist part, and the rentier part. Economists call this his 'theory of distribution'.

> ## KEY PASSAGE: THE LABOUR THEORY OF VALUE
>
> *The value of any commodity, therefore, to the person who possesses it, and who means not to use or consume it himself, but to exchange it for other commodities, is equal to the quantity of labour which it enables him to purchase or command. Labour, therefore, is the real measure of the exchangeable value of all commodities.*

o *Labour and exploitation:* Labour is the source of value – but there are others who exploit these labourers in their toil.

Smith describes the landlord as one who 'loves to reap where others have sowed'. 'They are the only one of the three orders whose revenue costs them neither labour nor care, but comes to them, as it were, of its own accord, and independent of any plan or project of their own.'

SUPPLY, DEMAND AND ALL-IMPORTANT WAGES

So Smith's economic analysis depends on a fourfold division (profit, rent, interest and capital) which seems to collapse into a twofold one (profit and capital). But there is another more serious problem, too: the old physical science problem of feedback. The price of say, nails, will depend on their 'usual price', the demand for things made using nails, the demand for other things made with nails, which are competing for the supply, the availability of iron to make nails and the people involved in making them and indeed all of these things may, in turn, be affected by the price of nails. When the price of a 'variable' depends on itself, we have what physicists term 'feedback'. Smith himself acknowledges that each factor, such as wages or rent, of the 'natural price' is in itself subject to the influence of demand in relation to supply. The amount of feedback with our example of the nails may not be very noticeable or significant, but consider the price of houses or postage stamps or shares! Feedback makes these phenomena behave strangely. In fact, this phenomenon of unpredictability or 'non-linearity' is what makes the stock markets possible. Because no one can predict anything reliably, it is always possible for someone to make a large profit by, say, speculating on the price of nails – the profit essentially coming out of the errors and miscalculations of others.

Smith accepts, certainly, that supply and demand are complex and cannot be represented by any simple (linear) relationship. Take the all-important matter of wages, for example. Wage levels vary:

> *Eighteen pence a day may be reckoned the common price of labour in London and its neighbourhood. At a few miles distance, it falls to fourteen and fifteen pence. Ten pence may be reckoned its price in Edinburgh and neighbourhood. At a few miles distance it falls to eight pence, the usual price of common labour... of the low country of Scotland... Such a difference in prices which is not always sufficient to transport a man from one parish to another, would necessarily occasions a great transportation of the most bulky commodities, not only from one parish to another, but from one end of the kingdom, almost from one end of the world, to the other, as would soon reduce them more nearly to a level. After all that has been said of the levity and inconstancy of human nature, it appears evidently that a man is of all sorts of luggage, the most difficult to be transported.*

And neither do variations in the price of labour correspond 'either in place or time' with those in the price of provisions, 'but they are frequently quite opposite'.

The only real component of wages, Smith says, is the amount necessary to keep the worker alive. (Actually, Smith does insist that the subsistence wage is actually a bit more – that which is consistent with common humanity.) If everyone had to do everything for themselves, as would be the case without the division of labour and the mechanisms for the trading or bartering of goods, people would all appear much the same too. Yet, people do in fact get paid very different amounts for jobs – and it is certainly not due to the different amount of time and effort invested. Although many spurious claims may be made to this effect, or about the rarity of the skills involved in certain kinds of work, Smith puts it this way:

KEY PASSAGE: THE EQUALITY OF TALENTS

The difference to Natural Talents in different men is, in reality, much less than we are aware of... [that] between a philosopher and a common street porter, for example, seem to arise not so much from nature as from habit, custom, and education. When they came into the world, and for the first six or eight years of that existence they were perhaps very much alike, and neither their parents nor play-fellows could perceive any remarkable differences...

---

o *'The difference...'*: Here we might embellish Smith's system, with the general rule that the more people are paid, the more important and unique they believe themselves to be.

However, whatever the truth about people's 'natural talents', in a growing economy, there may be a shortage of workers, obliging the employers to compete amongst each other for the workers, particularly by raising wages. Smith compares the experience of the then 'tiger' economies of Britain and America with the static economy of China, and the shrinking one of Bengal, concluding that it 'is not the actual greatness of national wealth, but its continual increase, which occasions a rise in the wages of labour'. This improvement of the 'lower ranks' is not an 'inconveniencey' but a moral necessity, for no society can surely be flourishing and happy, when the greater part of the members are poor and miserable. 'It is but equity, besides, that they who feed, cloath and lodge the whole body of the people, should have such a share of the produce of their own labour as to be themselves tolerably well fed, cloathed and lodged.' However, in the absence of economic growth, Smith warns, wages will be forced down to that subsistence level.

Smith details the other components of wages, too.

* There is the 'unpleasantness' factor. Unpleasant work will be avoided if the worker can subsist without doing it, and therefore the employer must raise the wage to compensate. Smith assumes all work to be basically worse than not working – 'toil and trouble', an assertion which may not be absolutely true, (unemployment itself can be a heavy burden) but surely is a reasonable approximation.

* Secondly, work which requires skill or training is like work which requires an expensive machine – the cost of hiring a professional must reflect this. Smith thinks work which is irregular may attract an extra premium (although we might argue that this is clearly not the case with that epitome of low-paid work, picking harvests for farmers). Work requiring people to step back slightly from their own selfish interests, such as being a doctor, also needs to be given additional rewards.

* Jobs involving a calculation of risk, such as being a soldier, or even taking on difficult legal cases which require winning, may not obtain the extra premium that the market should determine, if everything were worked out logically.

This is because, Smith observes, people tend to be optimistic about their chances of success in life. In a lottery, for instance, the chances of winning may be slightly less than the chance of being run over getting the lottery ticket (to embellish his example). People will tend to feel optimistic and sure that this sort of reality does not apply to them. Indeed, they may behave irrationally by buying several tickets – irrationally, since even if they bought all the tickets in the lottery, they would still end up with less money than they had put in. Similarly, he notes, people will not pay a small premium for insurance against fire, because they believe that this misfortune will not befall them anyway. A lottery is a good example of how not to get a 'return' on your money. People don't seem to mind much. However, usually there must be a 'return'. Wages are a 'form of return' on labour – you put some work in and get some money back.

Rent is also a form of return in that, for example, a landowner will allow a farmer to use land and will get some payment 'in return'. Rent is 'surplus' as, after the transaction is completed, the landowner still has his or her land, has made no investment of his or her own, but now has additional wealth. As the *Wealth of Nations* puts it, (Those greedy) land owners are a group 'whose revenue costs them neither labour nor care, but comes to them, as it were, of its own accord'. On the other hand, profit is a type of return which comes to capitalists as a reward for the trouble taken, and risks incurred. If landlords are the villains, workers the hapless victims, the capitalists are the heroes in the *Wealth of Nations.*

Smith describes the capitalist's role thus:

As soon as stock [that is capital] has accumulated in the hands of particular persons, some of them will naturally employ it in setting to work industrious people, whom they will supply with materials and subsistence, in which to make a profit by the sale of their work, or by what either labour adds to the value of the materials.

Remarkably, even the physical money seems to have a preference for the capitalists over the landowners: '... stock and labour naturally seek the most advantageous employment. They naturally, therefore, resort as much as they can to the town, and desert the country.'

Smith explains economics in terms of the circulation of goods and materials, acted upon, as John Locke, too, had earlier said, by labour. But capital in society consists of several parts, and they need to be distinguished. Smith emphasizes the different characteristics of capital and income, and explains the significance of savings. He begins, as we have seen, by observing that capital is of two types, fixed and circulating. There is the kind of capital which sits in ordinary people's cupboards – clothes and crockery which has been purchased and is still useful. (The cupboard itself, of course, is also part of such a stock of capital.) The feature of this sort of capital is that it provides no revenue, although in a sense, it could do were it to reappear in a jumble sale or some such.

Then there is the sort of capital which is productive, for example, machinery in factories, but also perhaps land prepared for agricultural use, and indeed trained personnel. This kind of capital is called 'fixed capital'. Fixed capital is like the lathes in a factory, or the skills of their operators. Circulating capital is the profit from the selling of the products, as this profit can then be used to buy a new carriage for the factory's owner, which involves more profits for the carriage maker, and for all their suppliers too. Because of this, it is circulating capital that keeps the economy going, and only certain parts of the economy produce it. Civil servants, teachers and soldiers, for example, do not produce any circulating capital, although they may be useful for other reasons. (It could be said, indeed, that they may facilitate others in the making of circulating capital, thereby increasing the amount of circulating capital.) Certainly, however, Smith does have his eye on certain activities which he considers to be essentially worthless. The labour of the 'menial servant', such as that of a footman who puts his master's coat on him each morning, he says, ' does not fix or realise itself in any particular or vendible commodity. His services generally perish in the very instant of their performance, and seldom leave any trace or value behind them...'.

The same goes, Smith carries on dismally, for some of the 'gravest and most important, and some of the most frivolous professions... Like the declamation of the actor, the harangue of the orator, or the tune of the musician, the work of all of them perishes in the very instant of its production.' (We must leave aside speculation as to whether Smith would have considered the advent of sound and video recording technology to make the professions any the less transitory and frivolous, but indubitably the entertainments industry today is now a major source of circulating capital.)

But then Smith, as we have seen, is really rather against spending in general (let alone on frivolities which he sees as usually unnecessary and inferior to saving). Money saved is available for business to borrow, creating new jobs which in turn creates new goods and new profits. These new profits more than cover the initial borrowings, creating 'a perpetual fund for the maintenance of an equal number in times to come'. The urge to save, Smith thinks, is 'the desire of bettering our condition, a desire which, though generally calm and dispassionate, comes with us from the womb, and never leaves us till we go into the grave.'

It is circulating capital that is the mark of the true capitalist as well as the stuff that powers the economy. Smith separates this in turn into three elements:

KEY DEFINITION:
THE THREE ELEMENTS OF CIRCULATING CAPITAL

* That all-important thing – money.
* The stocks of goods – manufactured in factories or grown on farms – available but not yet sold.
* The stock of raw materials and partially completed products owned by merchants, mine owners and farmers.

Of money, Smith adds:

The sole use of money is to circulate consumable goods. By means of it, provisions, materials and finished work, are bought and sold, and distributed to their proper consumers. The quantity of money therefore, which can be annually employed in any country must be determined by the quantity of the consumable goods which can be annually circulated within it.

THE CIRCULATION OF MONEY

Capitalism can be seen as a series of flows of money; income is exchanged for commodities reducing the amount of money in circulation. At the same time, a continuous process of replacement is taking place as new machines and raw materials are added, and new commodities procured. The system is self-correcting. When the market price is higher than the natural price, the prospect of easy profits encourages more people to produce the commodity. Supply begins to exceed demand, and competition amongst the vendors means prices drop. If the price drops below the cost of production, then people stop making the commodity, reducing supply, and the process reverses. Of course, another possibility is that the manufacturers cut their costs – perhaps through reducing wages, or perhaps by investing in superior manufacturing systems – in which case the price remains lower.

The same sort of natural balance that applies in the price of products applies to overall production in a country and to wage levels there. Even if:

… the profusion of government must undoubtedly have retarded the natural progress of England towards opulence and improvement, it has not been able to stop it. The annual produce of its land and labour is, undoubtedly, much greater at present than it was either at the restoration

or at the revolution. The capital, therefore, annually employed in cultivating this land, and in maintaining this labour, must likewise be much greater. In the midst of all the exactions of government, this capital has been silently and gradually accumulated by the private frugality and good conduct of individuals, by their universal, continual and uninterrupted effort to better their own condition. It is this effort, protected by law and allowed by liberty to exert itself in the manner that is the most advantageous, which has maintained the progress of England towards opulence and improvement in almost all former times, and which it is to be hoped will do so in all future times.

Notes to Chapter 5

Natural and actual prices are to be found in Book I, Chapter vii. The discussion of wages takes us into Chapter viii. In Chapter vi Smith explains the work of capitalists, and by Chapter x we see why money prefers capitalist to landowners. The 'great wheel of circulation' is described in Book II, Chapter iii.

The quotations from *Capital* (using the conventional indexing) are from I, 34 and I, 26, respectively.

6 Conclusion: Smith's Legacy

Smith saw the nature of theorizing, for example, about the stars and planets in his paper *On Astronomy*, as a series of 'paradigm shifts' to borrow Thomas Kuhn's later term. Theories are clung to even as they become increasingly complicated, in a futile bid to accommodate new information and data. But people are reluctant to abandon the current orthodoxy, and it requires something a bit shocking to come along before a new model is adopted, in turn to be modified and dropped. In this, Smith anticipates even the abandonment of Newtonian Absolute Space and Absolute Time, which shows his great open-mindedness.

But Smith's system is an economic one. *The gravitational force in the economy is the pull of self-interest.* Smith overestimates the pull of the force, writing that the natural price depends directly and solely on the three factors of cost. The market price reflects demand, that is 'effectual' demand. In a famine, demand for food may be high, but most are unable to offer any money for it. The price people will pay for something depends on how much they want it. But the price the product must be sold at depends on demand and several more cost factors: workers, that is the wages of the workers needed to produce it: machines, that is the profit of the owners of the capital or stock used; and the landowners, and the rent on the land or building.

The ordering of the chapters in his books reflects Smith's view of the importance and explanatory role of the concepts. So, the first chapter of the *Wealth of Nations* is entitled: 'Of the Division of Labour'; while the first chapter of *The Theory of Moral Sentiments* is entitled 'Of Sympathy'. However, there is also another kind of 'division of labour', in the dividing of society into the three great tribes: workers, employers and (land) owners. One notable consequence of the division of labour is that everyone has to acquire their needs though exchange. This leads Smith to the consideration of money, prices and the workings of the market.

THE CONTRADICTORINESS CHARGE

Some scholars have seen a contradiction between the altruism of the 'sympathetic' motivation, advanced in the *Moral Sentiments*, and the selfishness advanced in the *Wealth of Nations*. Smith says both are the glue of society. This charge, like the most successful critiques, works by a subtle sleight of hand which completely misrepresents the target's opinion. For Smith's system relies above all else on co-operation. It is a co-operation all the more powerful because it is unconsidered, hidden and forgotten. The butcher and the baker are working co-operatively, just as they are working for their own self-interest. Smith's emphasis on the role of property is more akin to Marxism's materialist explanation of social life, than it is to do with the posturing of today's state-centred political parties.

Smith is not wholly enamoured with the division process, however, (perhaps again recalling the specialists at Oxford) noting that a worker reduced to performing one task can become 'as stupid and ignorant as it is possible for a human creature to become' – even threatening to reduce people to 'riot and debauchery'. To combat this unfortunate tendency (amongst other reasons), Smith says the State should provide basic education for all citizens. 'For a very small expense the public can facilitate, can encourage, and can even impose upon almost the whole body of the people, the necessity of acquiring those most essential parts of education.'

TWO AIMS OF *WEALTH OF NATIONS*

The *Wealth of Nations* has two quite different parts. The first is an *analysis*, or 'model' of how the economy worked in Smith's day. The second is a *vision* of how to make it better – policy recommendations. Smith's policy is quite simple, *laissez-faire*: let the market decide.

However, this is not an entirely 'hands off', amoral policy. Smith is, remember, a highly moral writer. 'Our merchants and master manufacturers complain much of the bad effects of high wages in raising the price, and thereby lessening the sale of the goods both at home and abroad. They say nothing concerning the bad effects of high profits. They are silent with regard to the pernicious effects of their own gains. they complain only of those of other people.'

Smith's choice of examples is of humble objects destined for the masses not for the rich elites. This is not just an egalitarian flourish – it is an illustration of another fact – the engine of the economy is a mass production of humble goods for the common people – that is the source ultimately of the wealth of the few which may or may not then go on luxuries. (The pin itself is an unusual, indeed a feminized example. In fact, it might very well be made by women rather than the men Smith describes.)

The interests of the dealers, however:

... in any particular branch of trade or manufacture, is always in some respects different from, and even opposite to, that of the publick. To widen the market and to narrow the competition is always the interest of the dealers. To widen the market may be agreeable enough to the interest of the publick, but to narrow the competition must always be against it, and can serve only to enable the dealer, by raising their profits above what they naturally would be to levy, for their own benefit, an absurd tax upon the rest of their fellow citizens.

This leads on to Smith's recommendations for political and economic policy. Book V is devoted to the problem of how to raise money for the minimum essential State, and how to pay for the national debt, then, as now, a topic of great concern to the chattering classes. As to taxation, Smith offers three principles.

FAIR TAXES

Taxes should:

* take account of ability to pay and not be arbitrary – people should know what their liability will be if they do such and such

* be collected at the convenience of the tax-payer, not the collector; and

* be as efficient and economical as possible, not creating a dis-incentive to production in the first place.

These sound principles were not particularly novel to Smith. Francis Hutcheson and Sir James Steuart had said much the same just a few years earlier, but then that is to be expected with principles aiming to have, as Smith puts it, 'evident justice and utility'.

Today we might add a fourth and fifth principle of proportionality and choice: taxes should not be levied on essentials, such as food or water, neither should they be so great as to be effectively punishments for an activity, for example, smoking or drinking alcohol. Environmentalists might additionally append this with a sixth principle of 'encouraging sustainability' and avoiding damage to the ecology of the country.

Smith, as we saw in Chapter 1, was a great admirer of Quesnay, the French physician who had made a careful examination of the human body and had come up with an explanation of the function and role of the circulation of the blood. Smith himself was interested not in the makings of individual human bodies, but in the mechanism comprising what Thomas Hobbes, a hundred years earlier, had dubbed 'that Great Leviathan' – the State. Quesnay's great contribution to the theory of human biology was to discern the central role of the circulatory system which links all the organs of the body together in mutual dependence. So perhaps Smith's great contribution to the study of economics is his exposition of the circular role of money in the economy, which links all the parts of the State together in equal dependency.

Even so, Smith's theory of the wealth of nations remains fundamentally as it was originally intended: a model, to be abandoned as and when it ceases to be adequate to explain the complexity of reality.

REFERENCES AND FURTHER READING

There are many editions of the *Wealth of Nations* currently available, as discussed in the introduction earlier. Some of the most popular are the Kathryn Sunderland (Editor) edition for Oxford University Press (1993); the so-called *Glasgow Edition of the Works and Correspondence of Adam Smith: II: An Inquiry into the Nature and Causes of the Wealth of Nations* edited by W. B. Todd (1982) edition, also for OUP; the Hackett Publishing Co, Inc, (1993) edition and so on.

The correspondence of Adam Smith (including some little know gems) is published in a hefty collection by that name by Liberty Fund Inc, editors E.C. Mossner and I.S. Ross (1989) who also produce an edition of the *Lectures on Rhetoric and Belles Lettres*, edited by J.C. Bryce (1985) and of the *Lectures on Jurisprudence*, edited by J.L. Meek), D.D. Raphael (Editor), P.G. Stein (1982). Both Liberty (edited by D.D. Raphael and A.L. Macfie, 1984) and Prometheus Books have editions of *The Theory of Moral Sentiments'* (Paperback – January 2000).

W. P. D. Wightman has collected Smith's various *Essays on Philosophical Subjects* (including those *On Astronomy*) together, for Liberty Fund again (1982). The best way to locate Smith in his social and philosophical context is to read Pluto Press's excellent: *Political Philosophy form Plato to Chairman Mao* (2001), by (coincidentally enough!) one Martin Cohen.

The present work points towards some possible criticisms of Smith, but for a more trenchant attack on Smith and his mores the reader is offered Kenneth Lux's hardback *Adam Smith's Mistake*, published by Rider (1980). Lux argues that self-interest does not lead to a good society, but instead to social strife, ecological damage and abuse of power.

Emma Rothschild's popular new work, *Economic Sentiments: Adam Smith, Condorcet, and the Enlightenment* (Harvard, 2001) couched in non-specialist language offers another perspective on Adam Smith also.

Lastly, Jerry Z. Muller's *Adam Smith in His Time and Ours* (Princeton reprint edition 1995) reinstates Smith as part of a larger 'civilizing project' designed to create a more decent society.

FURTHER READING:

Life and Work

Ian Simpson Ross, *The Life of Adam Smith* (Oxford University Press/Clarendon, 1995)

D.D. Raphael, *Adam Smith* (Oxford University Press/Past Masters, 1985 – reprinted in *Three Great Economists*, 1997)

Thomas Wilson and Andrew Skinner (eds), *Essays on Adam Smith* (Oxford University Press, 1975)

Economics

Maurice Brown, *Smith's Economics* (Routledge, 1988)

J. Viner, *Essays on the Intellectual History of Economics*, ed. D. Irwin (Princeton University Press, 1991)

Mark Blaug, *Economic Theory in Retrospect* (Cambridge, 1978, Cha.2)

Cultural contexts

S. Copley and K. Sutherland (eds) Adam *Smith's Wealth of Nations: New Interdisciplinary Essays* (Manchester: Manchester University Press, 1995)

Vivienne Brown, *Smith's Discourse* (Routledge, 1994)

Martin Cohen, *Political Philosophy: from Plato to Chairman Mao* (Pluto, 2001)

Charles L. Griswold *Adam Smith and the Virtues of Enlightenment* (Cambridge University Press, 1999)

Adam Smith, *The Theory of Moral Sentiments* is accessible in an edition from Prometheus Books, 2000. That text, along with letters and other works such as 'The History of Astronomy' are included in the Glasgow Edition of the Works and Correspondence of Adam Smith (Oxford University Press, 1976-83)

INDEX